When Illness Comes

When Illness Comes
Seeking Strength through Prayer

Margaret Anne Huffman

Judson Press ® Valley Forge

Judson Press, © 1995
Valley Forge, PA 19482-0851

Scripture quotations in this volume are from:

The Revised Standard Version of the Bible (RSV), copyright © 1946, 1952, 1971, by the Division of Christian Education of the National Council of the Churches of Christ in the USA. Used by permission.

The New American Standard Bible (NASB), © 1960, 1962, 1963, 1968, 1971, 1972, 1973, 1975, 1977 by The Lockman Foundation. Used by permission.

The Living Bible (TLB), copyright © 1971. Used by permission of Tyndale House Publishers, Inc., Wheaton, IL. 60189. All rights reserved.

The New Revised Standard Version of the Bible (NRSV), copyright 1989 by the Division of Christian Education of the National Council of the Churches of Christ in the USA. Used by permission. All rights reserved.

The Holy Bible, King James Version (KJV).

The *Good News Bible* (GNB), the Bible in Today's English Version. Copyright © American Bible Society, 1976. Used by permission.

The New King James Version (NKJV). Copyright © 1972, 1984 by Thomas Nelson Inc.

HOLY BIBLE: New *International Version* (NIV), copyright © 1973, 1978, 1984. Used by permission of Zondervan Bible Publishers.

Library of Congress Cataloging-in-Publication Data
Huffman, Margaret Anne.
    When illness comes : seeking strength through prayer / Margaret Anne Huffman.
    p   cm.
    ISBN 0-8170-1232-X (pbk. : alk. paper)
    1. Sick—Prayer—books and devotions—English. I. Title.
    BV270.H84 1995
    242'.4—dc20   95-11991

Printed in the U.S.A.   95 96 97 98 99 00 01 02   8 7 6 5 4 3 2 1

For Gary

"... this is my beloved, and this is my friend ..."
(Song of Solomon 5:16, KJV)

Lynn, Rob, Beth, the enrichment

and

... for Aaron and Kali, to begin with

Contents

Preface
A Hand in the Night

"Night is coming . . ." (John 9:4b, NRSV).

We never know when night is coming, for night can come boldly in a faltering heart, the ringing of a phone, or a wailing siren. It can come stealthily in a cluster of runaway cells, a long-feared diagnosis, a progression of pain.

Thrust into the dark night of illness, perhaps of dying, we as the patient, family, or friend are left to watch and wait, to worry. But we are not alone.

These prayers are gleaned from my nights as family, friend, patient, minister's wife, and newspaper reporter covering health issues. They lift us, no matter where night overtakes us, into God's waiting hands where we will be held, our concerns shared. And once there, we will discover that night's dark moments become lighter, more hopeful, when holding hands with one another, with God the link between.

To God, the Great Physician, there is no situation so traumatic *or* so trivial that it is beyond God's healing compassion and desire for us to use prayer as a resource in responding to it; no prayer is unacceptable. Sometimes the only prayers we can offer are our fears and angers; God welcomes them, too.

May these prayers be a bridge from isolation to an awareness of God's presence and availability. For no matter how bleak the spaces between wellness and illness, life and death, we are not alone; always God's hand is outstretched for us to grasp.

I am grateful to those who opened their hands to me, inspiring my words: Mary Hopkins, R.N., oncology; Mary Kay Hart, hospice volunteer; the Rev. Gary Huffman; the Rev. Dr. Jack Skiles; John R. Hayes, M.D.; Kevin Stamm, M.D.; and especially the patients and families.

Introduction
Hand in Hand

We are holding out our hands, Lord, to receive comfort, for illness is rerouting life and reminding us how frail we truly are. We are holding out our hands to receive answers to the "why" questions: "Why now?" "Why us?" "Why this way?" We are holding out our hands for maps to the next spot on our journey through this dark valley of illness . . . even of dying.

We feel your warm handclasp of companionship and now hold out our hands for one another, seeking their support and their companionship, too.

Thank you for your gift of hands, blessed resources for us that:
- give steadying support beneath our elbows;
- bind up and cure, patch and fix;
- rub backs and feverish brows; ladle pills and healing potions;
- hold and pat ours in friendship, love, companionship;
- greet us on visits; pat our shoulders in encouragement;
- encircle us in sympathy and a consoling embrace;
- stir up nourishing foods to sustain and treats to entice;
- applaud efforts made toward recovery;
- play a hymn of celebration for reprieve on piano, fiddle, drum;
- lay on to petition, to heal; and
- in time wave us on to the distant shore where you wait.

Wherever we are on this path of illness, Lord, we know your strong hand is there to guide and to hold us.

Words to Hold You: "Though I walk in the midst of trouble . . . thou dost stretch out thy hand . . . thy right hand delivers me. . . . thy steadfast loves endures forever. Do not forsake the work of thy hands" (Psalm 138:7-8, RSV).

When Illness Comes . . .

"Though I walk in the midst of trouble . . .
you stretch out your hand . . .
your right hand delivers me."

We are holding out our hands, Lord,
to receive comfort.

We are holding out our hands to receive answers.

Wherever we are on this path of illness,
we know your strong hand
is there to guide and to hold us.

ABC of Prayer

Like a bullet, illness has hit me smack dab between the eyes. As I tremble in its wake, I find myself down on knees that have not knelt in prayer for a while.

Am I too late? Do you hear returning prayers? Is there room for newcomers? Will I be penalized for not being one of the regulars?

I know the answer from what others say, even if I've not needed you very much, nor believed. I confess I may still have a fair share of doubts. Nevertheless, Lord, I—we—feel welcomed.

Yet now that I am here, God, I don't know *how* to pray. Translate my tongue-tied thoughts into prayer, for I am like the child who recited the alphabet during prayer time at church, explaining, "I don't know how to pray, I just know the letters of the alphabet. If I send them all to God, then I know God can arrange them in my prayer."

So here I am, doubled over in worry about my illness, and all I can pray are thoughts as jumbled as that child's alphabet. Arrange them into my prayer; I—we—have that child's trust you can do it.

Like children, we will be practicing forming letters into words into prayers, understanding now that *all we think and feel at all times*—not just formally on our knees with hands folded and eyes closed—*can be prayer.*

I feel better having had this conversation and am sorry it's taken so long to find my way here. Thank you for listening. I will be back with new alphabet jumbles for you to help me sort out.

Words to Hold You: ". . . unless you are converted and become like children, you shall not enter the kingdom of heaven" (Matthew 18:3 NASB).

Odds-on Favorite

I'm going to beat the odds, Lord, beat this disease, beat the gloom that fills my room where doomsayers wring their hands over me.

I've neither time nor interest in that, for I'm also told there are certain odds my disease can be beaten. So why not be one of those who beats it? There are faces behind those winning numbers, so why can't one be mine?

Riddles about "glasses half full or half empty" are easily answered, for my glass is so full it's overflowing with hope and determination. I see myself linking up with you, one hand on the hem of your robe, the other holding onto whatever pills and potions the doctor offers. I hear myself shouting, "Hallelujah!" at the good news I'll be getting one day about a for-sure reprieve, a clean bill of health at a three-, five-, ten-and-more-year checkup. It's got to happen to somebody, Lord; why not me?

It will, Lord, it will; for like sheep eating grass in the greenest of green pastures, you and I will have gotten rid of the runaway cells in my body. Thou will indeed lead me through the valley.

Words to Hold You: ". . . my flesh also will abide in hope" (Acts 2:26, NASB).

Where Is God's Will?

Is my illness your will, God?

It's a riddle and I need answers, for I want you to help me heal. But if you *sent* this illness, how can I trust you to do that?

And, O Creator of all natural order, what about the innocent? the teetotaling liver-cancer patient and the athlete with a diseased heart? stillborn babies and stricken-down toddlers? those who eat properly, exercise, pray, brush, and floss? Why is disease in their bodies despite the reverence they've given them? Did you will their disease? mine?

No, *none* of the maladies are your will; *none* of this suffering is your design, even when we contribute to our illnesses. We hear you weeping with us and our families; we feel your hand on our shoulders as you tend to us in the ambiguity of living a mortal life. You don't will bad things; you will only the best. And when that isn't possible in the randomness of nature, you are here with us as we suffer.

Thank you for your presence. Forgive our easy blame of you. Forgive us for even considering that any Parent would deliberately hurt one of his very own children. What could you possibly have to gain?

O God, freed from fear of you, I feel myself getting stronger as your healing energy flows through me, restoring me to my abundant life, your original intention for all your children.

Words to Hold You: "Which of you, if his son asks for . . . a fish, will give him a snake? . . . how much more will your Father in heaven give good gifts to those who ask him!" (Matthew 7:9-11, NIV). "I have come that they may have life, and that they may have it more abundantly" (John 10:10, NKJV).

Give Me Courage

I know how the Cowardly Lion felt in "The Wizard of Oz," for I, too, lack courage. This illness has reduced me to a quivering coward, Lord.

I am afraid I won't be able to make it through this illness, treatment, and changed life that follows. *If* it follows, for I am also afraid of what might happen no matter how reassuring and optimistic others are.

I am afraid of pain, of being dependent, of having no control of either my body or surroundings. I need a strong dose of courage.

Help me understand, Lord, that the courage I am praying for is not dry-eyed stoicism and perky denial. Courage is not hiding my feelings, even from you, and putting on a brave false face.

How marvelous that your gift of courage translates *wishing* into *hoping*, the active word we need to help us get well; it translates fear into energy and sadness into resolve. It takes courage to heal, for sometimes it's easier to simply sit still, stay afraid, and feel powerless.

It is courageous to be afraid, Lord, for fear is honest; so is anger, disappointment, grief. Help us recognize feelings as potential fuel that can be turned into weapons for fighting illness once they are redeemed by you.

Send me the courage to heal; redeem my cowardly worries and give me your hand for the journey toward recovery. Through your grace, I have courageously faced *what is* and am now off to see *what can be*.

Words to Hold You: "Be strong and courageous. . . . He will not fail you or forsake you" (Deuteronomy 31:6, NASB).

Why Me?

Why me, Lord? Why me?
I raise my fist to you in defiance if this is your will. I have a bad illness; the waiting to find out how bad is just beginning. *Why me?*
This prayer is a diary. I can only write the beginning because I am so angry. I lie awake afraid you will be disappointed in my anger, my lack of faith, my insistence I should be spared. But shouldn't everyone?
Why me, Lord? Why me?
I raise my hand to you in petition; hold it between yours so I can feel your warmth; I have none of my own. Be with me during tests, treatment. Be with my doctors, with my family, who would take my place if they could.

Why me, Lord? Why me?
I raise my hand in victory—not because my prognosis is OK, but because I am. How do I know I am OK? Because I'm not alone. Like a pearl of great value, a sheep of your fold, I know you have come to find me. Because I know I am a child of yours, loved and known even to the number of hairs on my head. Because I know you will always be with me as you are now. I recognize you in the eyes of my doctor; I feel you in the arms of my family.
And now, O God, I ask you this time from my knees, *Why me?* What is there you need me to do so that I was spared? where? I ask again, but now from my newfound willingness to go with you, *why me?*

Words to Hold You: "Out of the depths I cried to Thee. . . . For with the LORD there is lovingkindness . . ." (Psalm 130: 1,7, NASB).

The Swing Tree

All my life, God, I've been the strong one. I've acted like I was both a strong, sturdy tree my family and friends could shelter beneath as well as a "swing tree" to hold myself up like a child in a swing.

I've not wanted to burden anyone else, yet once in awhile and especially now, I need to be held up by someone else's strength and "swing from another branch," for it is lonely being strong.

And now illness is making me weak in both body and spirit, and I *can't* be strong all by myself anymore. Is it healthy to keep all this fear and need inside? But now everyone is counting on my being "strong"—even nurses and doctors; I've trained everyone well!

Yet what a helpful resource I am cheating myself out of by staying isolated in false strength. Perhaps real strength is in learning to ask for help. Teach me how, O God; help me learn to graciously accept it when offered.

I feel secure learning to turn myself over to the caregiving of others, for yours are the first hands I've grabbed. I know I can let go now of "acting strong" because you are strong enough for both of us.

Being held by you, God, I feel like a child swinging gently from the branches of a sturdy oak tree, moving beyond this stuck spot of illness to get well. No one need be his or her own "swing tree" when you are so close by.

Words to Hold You: *"I will say to the LORD, 'My refuge and my fortress . . .'" (Psalm 91:2, NASB).*

A Silent Partner

Few of us knew how to be ill, Lord, or that illness would be so noisy. I never did. In the midst of constant questions, speculations, and the daily buzz of routine, I need to be quiet. I need a silent partner who will come and simply sit beside me; there are times when silence is golden.

Sometimes when family and friends fill the room, they talk, talk, talk without saying anything or talk only about themselves. Worse, they don't listen to what *I* am saying, especially when I speak with my heart, not just my mouth. It's as if they fear silence is scary, but it's not.

Remind *me* not to chatter and fill in quiet spots either, Lord, for to be quiet is restorative, like resting beside still waters. Help those who visit to understand this too, and know sometimes I just want them to sit nearby quietly while I doze.

When we're ill, be our constant, silent Partner, so when we need to talk, we will always have someone at our elbow to listen; when we need to be still, we will know you are still at our elbow, only now as a quiet Companion in the silence. It is welcome in this chattering course of illness.

Words to Hold You: "For thus said the Lord GOD . . .,
'in quietness and in trust shall be your strength'"
(Isaiah 30:15, RSV).

Poor Me

Loving God, despite my stiff upper lip and brave face in the midst of this illness, inside I am feeling very, very sorry for myself.

But who wouldn't if they had to suffer what I am? I feel terrible and am sick of feeling terrible, worried, and limited.

Sit with me while I whine. Hold me closely as I go down my long list of complaints without being the least bit reasonable. I am sick of being reasonable. I am sick of being cheered up. I am sick of being scolded, "Others have heavier burdens." Mine are heavy enough, thank you.

Accept our grumpy selves when it comes to this, for they are all we have to bring you right now. Talking helps—releasing toxic dregs of misery—and we feel better afterward. Help us to not get stuck here, for self-pity distorts our perspective and we can't see the healing resources being offered in the hands of others: medicine, therapies, companionship.

God, help us to move beyond self-pity just as we move from bed to chair to walker to our own two feet and on out the sickroom door. Help us to look outside our bodies, outside the world of illness, and back into the world of health, vigor, and the rest of life.

I feel you gently pulling me toward it as children do when they tug on my hands to come play. I want to, Lord, so cure me of this tempting chronic self-absorption, for it is a deadly virus that can paralyze my soul.

Words to Hold You: "No one cares for me" (Psalm 142:4b, GNB).

Get a Grip

I have lost control of my life, Lord. I am frantic to get a grip wherever I can on this slippery slope of illness. Being sick has torn my hands loose from their casual hold on routine, assumptions, and the future.

I feel as if I am falling down a mountain with nothing familiar to grasp. Chaos, like loose stones sliding beneath my feet, is everywhere. This illness is the biggest thing wrestling control from me; like an octopus it tugs with questions, pain, treatments, and uncertainties. I can't control its course, much less its outcome, and am terrified it will control me like the tail wagging the dog.

When moments like these overwhelm, help us find even small ways to regain a sense of holding the reins to what happens next. *Control* is as elusive as clutching an ice cube; your gift of *directing* is better to use, Lord, like a conductor directing an orchestra, not controlling the music.

By letting go of control, we'll have energy to assume some leadership in our recovery, working alongside doctor, nurse, medicine, and family and friends' support, knowing you are central to the process.

As a parent places a hand around a child's hand to show how to use baseball bat, tennis racket, or pencil, I feel your hand on my hand, Lord, showing me how to direct my life, even on this new, chaotic journey.

Words to Hold You: "Cast your burden upon the LORD, and He will sustain you" (Psalm 55:22, NASB).

Homesick

God of patience, I want out of this sickbed. I want to go home and back to my regular life. I want to lie in the slight hollow of my own bed where I nest; I want to sink into my favorite chair that encircles me just right, like a hug.

I want to stroke the fur of my cat, pat the dog, and hear birds outside my window. Even starlings sing a beautiful song when you've not heard any birds for a while.

I want to eat from my own dishes, drink from my favorite mug, dry on a real towel after a real bath. I'm sure I'll get better faster once I'm back home again, Lord. Can I find the means to make it possible?

Help me find products, devices, and people to help send me home. Help me find ways to afford it, for my spirit cannot afford homesickness.

Help me get well enough to make the homebound journey soon. If it's not possible right now, send me home in my thoughts and dreams.

Dozing a bit now, I can feel my favorite quilt settling across my shoulders and I snuggle into its familiar smells and texture. I can see the patterns on wallpaper, path on carpets; I can smell the special fragrances of each room.

Thank you, God, for a glimpse of home. I'm working on getting there for real, and I can rest better now at least dreaming of being *Home, Sweet, Home*. Let's hold that thought. It's enough until we get there.

Words to Hold You: "In peace I will both lie down and sleep, For Thou alone, O LORD, dost make me to dwell in safety" (Psalm 4:8, NASB).

Frozen Assets

God, remember the days when I was angry things wouldn't stay the same? The car wouldn't stay clean, golf swing stay straight, checkbook stay balanced? My big frustration was how changeable, inconsistent life was.

How foolish, for now everything is consistent—consistently frozen, from my body to my view and options. Paralyzed by an alphabet soup of illness, a stroke of misfortune, I'll be consistently unchangeable.

Now what do I do? I fear dependency. I fear living, for this isn't living by my standards. I fear dying. Even my spirit and soul are frozen.

Help me to grieve and go on . . . go on in new ways you will reveal to me as I make my faltering way as far as I can. Hold me while I name and mourn all I have lost, weeping and wailing like the abandoned child I feel I am. Then, with you to lean on, I will focus on what I have left.

Show me others who paint with their teeth or toes, people who write with puffs of breath on a machine, who talk with blinks of an eye. No, Lord, no, this is not good enough, but it is better than my immobile spirit.

Help me graciously accept others' help and not always act self-sustained, self-controlled, for I can't afford that luxury. Send caregivers who'll keep me at my best and independent of mind and spirit if not body.

Help me to not put on a brave false face, but rather keep an honest one like yours. You aren't telling me this will be easy, Lord, just possible.

Words to Hold You: "'. . . with God all things are possible'" (Matthew 19:26, NASB).

Bouquets of Love

Sometimes, Lord, our very best selves return to us spit-shined in the reflection of other people's love of us. And as sick as we are, as moody and grumpy, that's amazing.

I feel cherished and loved from the efforts others make on my behalf. I gain strength from their messages in mysterious ways. I feel them helping me to recover and regain strength, purpose, will.

Do those who write or come calling realize how important their efforts are? Do they realize how even the smallest gesture can divide sick days into light and darkness? Do they know how their support lifts and encourages?

Remind us to tell them how much they matter, that whatever they bring along or send—cards, notes, flowers, balloons, things to eat, things to read, things to watch, things to think about—lifts our spirits higher than the highest balloon!

Remind us later to go see or at least call or send cards to everyone we know who has so much as even a sniffle! We all need to feel important and that others are helping in our healing.

I am grateful that you are my first caller each day I am ill, bringing large bouquets of love that overflow far beyond my sickroom.

Consider this a thank-you note, Lord. I've many more to do.

Words to Hold You: "This is how we know what love is: . . . our love should not be just words and talk; it must be true love, which shows itself in action" (1 John 3:16-18, GNB).

A Package Deal

Does getting old always mean getting sick, Lord?

I'm laid up right now and worrying about this, for I'm getting older and collecting aches, pains, and new ailments like pebbles in a pocket. We seniors dread getting sick—sicker—with old folks' ailments, fearing we have "one foot in the grave and the other on a banana peel" just because we're old and are sick right now.

Slow our anxieties and quiet our frustrations, for aging and illness are not a package deal. Remind us that illness can be an opportunity to shape up and skip out of lethargy, poor habits, and unfit attitudes that can make us far sicker than can mere passing years.

Give those of us with silvering hair the good sense to elude further illness by diligent self-care. Remind us to take a good look at what *we* can do to recover, even get better than we were before we got sick. We intend to be ready for any challenges our bodies may present.

This is a wake-up call too, reminding us to tend to our hearts that might be hardened, not sick. Help us to forgive and ask for forgiveness. Help us to speak of love and pleasure in others' company. Help us to not put off what we need to do to recover not only our body but our mind and soul too.

Pacemaker, walker, cane, pills, and replaced body parts— Lord, we're prepared to use them all with your steadying hand under our elbows if aging and illness insist on being companions! Here's to long life and good health; they go together so well, a package deal of gifts from your hand.

Words to Hold You: "He alone is my Rock, my rescuer, defense and fortress—why then should I be tense with fear when troubles come?" (Psalm 62:6, TLB).

Insufficient Funds

How am I going to pay for this illness, Lord? Even the cost of Band-Aids has gotten out of sight, those simple patches of healing prescribed, dispensed, charted, inventoried, reordered, charged, and itemized on hospital bills that are so infuriating to receive.

Retirement, savings, and sugar-bowl caches are depleted, Lord, and still we can't cover the cost of this last illness. Fear is a heartbreaking complication as we lie here recuperating while worrying about how we can afford the high cost of getting well.

It may seem trivial to fret the cost of Band-Aids during battles to save our lives. Medical marvels cost money, we know, and no matter the price tag we want them. But we are sick with worry about paying up.

Who *can* afford to get sick? Or better still, who can afford to get well? While some of us carry so many insurance policies it requires a briefcase to hold them, others of us carry only our bowed heads and sad stories to offer the clanging, unforgetting cash register.

Restore us to common sense so cures can be found for this epidemic of financial sickness. Be present in conversations about if and when to bring in expensive, high-tech measures to prolong life . . . death.

In the meantime, Lord, help me to figure out where I'm going to get a Band-Aid large enough to patch the hole this illness has made in my wallet.

Words to Hold You: "Say to him, 'Be careful, keep calm and don't be afraid'" (Isaiah 7:4, NIV).

Taking a Chance

We'll try anything, Lord, to boost our odds for recovery. We'll endure side effects and be guinea pigs for the simple chance to live longer. Most of our lives, we wanted certainty, but not now. Certainty means immediate death. Help us to find places where we can be part of trials, experiments, and test runs trying out technology, mechanical parts, and noxious pills and potions. We'll be better off on their roller coasters of uncertainty than doing nothing. Reassure us we are not being foolish to tell ourselves and our families that we're not ready to give up, for we aren't.

Guide us as pioneers who blaze trails of courage, bound to succeed no matter the outcome. Doing whatever we can to live makes us feel better no matter how sick we feel otherwise. In a footnote, we're grateful to add to knowledge, to others' chances, as we improve our own.

Bless and comfort our families in the grueling task of waiting; their support is life-sustaining. Bless the doctors, nurses, researchers, laboratory animals, and financial wizards who contrive to push medical care forward. Keep them diligent in keeping quality of life and patient wholeness as the top of all goals, Lord, for that patient is me.

And now we take our turn in the unknown. Be with us, Lord, as we summon courage to face its uncertainty in the name of progress, our own and others', for it's our best chance at life.

Words to Hold You: ". . . I have set before you life and death, blessing and curse; therefore choose life, that you and your descendants may live . . ." (Deuteronomy 30:19, RSV).

Living Will, Living Well

Being ill sets a person to thinking, Lord, so I am planning ahead.

Some shudder, but making a living will and preplanning my memorial are not morbid. I am simply crossing every "t" and dotting each "i" of my life. I know what hymns and Scripture verses I want; I know which treatments I will and won't allow before I reach that memorial moment.

I welcome discussion even if the family and I stumble a bit. We're not used to talking about these things as if they're OK. But what in your creation, wise Lord—even its leave-taking—is not OK? Help us to feel easier with it.

We will continue prayerfully negotiating with you, our doctors, the family, and ourselves on final details. Give us questions to ask and options to consider. Guide our hands as we sign on dotted lines. Tending to this feels tidy and loving of ourselves.

I'm doing this, too, because I want to be a caretaker for my family a last time. Sparing them decisions they are ambivalent about is my farewell gift. Now no one need worry about what happens next and who decides; you and I do, Lord, partners to the end.

To think of these things doesn't mean we're ungrateful for life; it means we're learning not to worship physical life but rather to worship you as our beginning *and* end, alpha *and* omega. We fear neither.

Words to Hold You: "For this great God is our God forever and ever. He will be our guide until we die" (Psalm 48:14, TLB).

Just the Facts

Just the facts, Lord, I want just the facts about this illness, suddenly the most important thought I have. The family wants facts too, so they can be my advocate and cheerleader armed with truth and options.

With knowledge we can be partners in care, better able to choose responses, muster energy. The more we know the less fearful and imaginative we will be. And you know how wild our imaginations can be! Help us learn what we need each step of the way, for being healed to the reality is a big step toward the rest of healing.

These are enlightened times, Lord, when illness is not something to be ignorant about or hide. Be with us as we run to medical books on library and bookstore shelves; steady our hands as we dial 800 numbers.

Give us words for questions and courage to ask them of our doctors. Remind them to be truthful and patient in the telling, for hope may be found in new answers. Speaking of doctors, Great Physician, remind us to seek second opinions, even third, until we find partners in our healing.

Keep us focused on educating ourselves, *not* to make paths through this illness that are chiseled in stone, but to become equipped like drivers wearing seat belts. Whatever facts we learn, your presence is the ever-present footnote.

Words to Hold You: "'Then you will know the truth, and the truth will set you free'" (John 8:32, NIV).

A Broken System, A Broken Heart

Should I sue? Should I report this doctor, tattling to a board of medical peers? What would they do if their mother had provided the punch line in the old joke, "By the time I get in to the doctor, I'll be dead!"

She was, Lord. Dead and buried before her appointment grudgingly made by a clogged system and its unreachable doctor for months later.

How, he challenged, was she going to pay? Besides, how could she expect to get in before others?

It was a reasonable expectation, for she suspected she was mortally ill. Many of us know when something is out of kilter in the marvelous body with which you endowed us; remind doctors of this, Lord.

My tale is one among many, and we worry that the health-care system is sickest of all. Give us wisdom to heal it.

While we're mending health care, remind physicians they can heal better as partners than as adversaries or unapproachable mechanics on schedules set to a ticking financial meter. Teach them to leave a few spaces in those schedules for the unexpected patient who wakes short of breath, doubled over in pain, terrified at the lump beneath a hand.

Thank you for the courage I needed to complain about our small corner of this mess. Were you as outraged as I when the bill arrived for Mother's missed appointment?

Most of all, thank you for the doctor who wasn't too busy to ease her suffering; that doctor is a healer in your tradition.

Words to Hold You: "Do not merely look out for your own personal interests, but also for the interests of others" (Philippians 2:4, NASB).

Lightning Strikes

Lightning struck one of the prize trees in the park where I walk, Lord. Its leaves are withering, and no one is sure it will survive the strike. I am sad each time I walk past.

Lightning has struck us, too, in this terrible, sudden illness of our special one, and we have no certain idea what will come next.

Why, why does lightning strike the strong and sturdy among us? Right next to the tree in the park is a straggly, falling-down, and unattractive tree; why didn't lightning strike it instead?

We confess we are looking in anger at the straggly among us. You know who, Lord—ones who don't value their lives or seem fit for living because they do so many mean things. Why weren't *they* struck by the lightning of illness?

We are ashamed of these thoughts but know it is best to get out *all* our feelings, even ugly ones. We know you are neither shocked nor disappointed in our rage, for you can bear all things, even our duality.

Reassure us that lightning is mostly as random as illness and you didn't send it to topple the patient, us, or the tree. Lightning just happens.

O God, it is a mixed-up time, and we are double-minded: angry at the world you created where lightning cannot be controlled any better than disease *and* gratefully greedy for the maximum days to spend in this world. Grant our loved one many days, never mind the threat of lightning. When it does strike, remind us to look for your rainbows.

Words to Hold You: "Wilt thou be to me like a deceitful brook, like waters that fail?" (Jeremiah 15:18b, RSV). "I set my bow in the cloud . . ." (Genesis 9:13, RSV).

Switching Places

Suddenly life is topsy-turvy, Lord, as illness reverses our roles. Now our take-charge leader is ill, dependent while we are changing oil in cars, paying bills, ferrying kids, cleaning gutters, and charting the rocky course through situations we'd never imagined we'd face; that was the other's job.

The worst moment is realizing we can't live by assumptions forever. Feelings of vulnerability creep up and down our spines like icy fingers of doom, for we've assumed roles and habits so long.

Are we equal to the task? Can we switch places for even a brief while? Is it only gloom from here on out? Are all assumptions gone?

Help us to reach into ourselves where we have resources like veins of gold not yet mined. They are *new* assumptions to live by: that we are resilient, adaptable, able, courageous, creative, and empowered by you.

Lord, remind us that through our strength at picking up the slack, we are helping to heal the one who is ill; without worrying about details they can focus on getting well, knowing we are OK. And we are.

Help us to be proud of achievement and to retain some of this newfound strength and knowledge of how to mine our resources when this crisis is passed, for we are stronger than we thought. This is a welcome discovery despite how we've had to learn it.

We assume, Lord, you'll provide us what we need, even a set of "do-it-yourself" directions for things we've never done before . . . but can do now.

Words to Hold You: "I do not consider that I have made it on my own; . . . forgetting what lies behind . . . , I press on . . ." (Philippians 3:13-14, RSV).

Third Time's Not a Charm

The illness has come back again, Lord—a relapse, a reoccurrence, and a reliving of the nightmare. We don't want to deal with it again. And again. And maybe yet again.

How selfish we feel. Forgive our doled-out loving. Redeem our anguish into something useful because guilt is compounding grief.

We don't have time for this interruption. It feels like having a blowout on the highway—a big bang, being dragged toward a ditch, and a big hole where whole, intact assumptions used to be. We are stranded.

Help us to see, though, that each relapse also brought more quality time. Each blowout got patched and took us all farther. That is the point to focus on now: more quality time, going on farther even on a spare.

This thought energizes us to cope with illness's return, function on less sleep and fewer assumptions, and not require that life be without blowouts and bumps before we consider it good enough to be grateful for.

It *is* good, Lord; life is very good. We celebrate now the possibility of even more to share with our special one who is also weary of the yo-yo.

Loving God, be with us in disappointment and exhaustion and as we secretly confess we want no more of this yo-yo. Having said that, we are filled with your Spirit, like retreaded tires, ready for the journey wherever it leads—up, down, and perhaps even back around again. We can make it.

Words to Hold You: "You were tired out by the length of your road, Yet you did not say, 'It is hopeless.' You found renewed strength, Therefore you did not faint"
(Isaiah 57:10, NASB).

Lost Shadows

We've lost our shadows, Lord, and are standing here like Peter Pan, who wanted someone to sew it back on; we feel as if we have no self left.

But we didn't lose our shadows, those reflections of our ordinary lives, in a make-believe story but rather in the worrying, exhausting time of this bedside vigil with our special one.

We look in a mirror and see no one recognizable: hollow-eyed, aged, moody, worn out. We are so fragile of body and faint of spirit that when we step into the sunlight, we cast no shadow.

And, really, Lord, we've lately not found much sunlight required to make shadows, for days of illness are full of darkness, the nights long. Help us to not lose ourselves in the worrying so that we wind up of no value in the healing process. We are needed here to be as whole as we can be.

So even though we might balk at the thought, send us outdoors to pick flowers, toss snowballs, walk in raindrops, or scuff through leaves. Bring us back to this bedside restored, whole again, and casting shadows of hope and energy strong and bold enough so that we can be of real help.

And remind us when we feel so small and helpless that we can make no shadow that we are never out of *your* light and warm presence. Send us promised reflections of ourselves restored, balanced, and equipped for yet more waiting, more worrying if that is to be.

And there, in the midst of these new images that we, like children playing "Hand Shadows on the Wall," now see reflected all around us, Lord, is the image of your hand holding ours, a life-sized truth.

Words to Hold You: "When anything is exposed by the light, it becomes visible . . ." (Ephesians 5:13, RSV).

Moody

We were unprepared for the roller coaster of moods we ride through illness and are dizzy with up-and-down, 'round-and-'round feelings. Moodiness is a symptom that patient and family share, Lord. Beware!

Ease our worries and encourage us to feel what we feel from one minute to the next whether it seems reasonable or not. We are like cranky children one minute and stern robots another and don't know which mood to trust! Remind us to trust all of them.

We are grateful that through your gracious gift of emotions and moods, it is not only OK to feel all of what we feel, but essential. No one feeling you have endowed us with is better than another. By feeling all, we will not get stuck in one. Striving for only one emotion is like making rainbows with only two colors, both gray!

No matter how down we may feel at this moment, Lord, we know from dizzying firsthand experience we'll soon be up again. As health returns, so, too, will balance and we won't feel as if we are falling off one side of the bed or the other!

Help us to imagine how it would appear on a monitor if our feelings were charted alongside our heartbeats. Hurrah! See those up-and-down squiggles? Hurrah! It's the flat lines we want to avoid, body and soul.

Words to Hold You: "We are afflicted in every way, but not crushed; perplexed, but not despairing" (2 Corinthians 4:8, NASB).

Double Whammy: Complications

Recovery was going well, Lord, when complications set in. Was it someone's fault? Were treatments, procedures incorrect? Was it avoidable?

We understand the frustration that leads to lawsuits, for we feel betrayed and cheated of the hard-won relief and joy we felt when the corner was turned and recovery seemed certain.

Enough is enough. We are fast running out of energy and patience to withstand both this illness and worries about it. Help us to move beyond feeling that this double whammy of trouble is personal.

Remind us that accidents can happen; treatments can backfire; procedures go awry; healers err. Help us to understand when healthy parts are harmed in the midst of the healing or when complications set in that life is "both/and," like a double-headed coin, in other areas as well: Our comfort and convenience, Lord, *can* lead to pollution; our food, to overweight and disease; our leisure, to laziness. Efforts made with good intentions *can* yield not-so-good results; it just happens.

Help us to recover from this double whammy within illness. Help these exhausting complications to be healed and our spirits restored to believe that none of this was intended to be; it just happened. Give us strength.

Words to Hold You: ". . . as we received mercy, we do not lose heart. . . . 'Light shall shine out of darkness . . .'" (2 Corinthians 4:1, 6-8, NASB).

Take a Break

How quickly the unbelievable becomes not only believable, Lord, but ordinary daily routine. How amazingly the unthinkable becomes the only thought we have: illness, illness, illness.

We think, talk, and dream about nothing else. Reeling from illness' blow to our special one and its pressure on us, we are about at the end of a very long rope. We can't carry on normal conversations, speaking only the jargon of symptoms and treatments. We sleep sitting up with one eye open, one ear attentive, if at all. We can't eat anything not fried up in a hurry to eat on the run.

We're shocked to emerge, like moles, outdoors in the sunshine. We are annoyed at others who go about their lives in sunshine routines that do not include illness. We are even angry at birds singing, people working, children playing, cars honking, friends calling.

We've had it.

Be with us, Lord, as we dangle here at the end our rope. Encourage us to hold on just an hour at a time, to go outdoors and bring sunshine back indoors with us, to seek out birds singing and people laughing, for we need balance as we swing to and fro on our rope at the whim of illness.

Most of all, Lord, guard our comings and goings, for tiredness creates carelessness. Protect *our* health as we push limits of endurance.

Words to Hold You: "He gives power to the faint . . ."
(Isaiah 40:29, RSV).

Turnaround

I'm frantically looking for you, Lord, but can't find you around this last turn where illness has taken a turn for the worse. Where are you?

Everyone thought healing was possible and that life could hold both quality and quantity, but now no one is certain. Why have you left us?

Are you guiding this misdirection, Lord? Are you sitting wherever you sit watching us and saying, "Since they've handled this so well, I'll test them a bit more and see how they do with *this*"? Are you plotting more tests of faith to see how long we can stay faithful?

Some say so, knowing you as a bully with endless butterflies from which to pluck wings or a teacher of trick questions for us to always fail.

But even in my blindest moment I know you are worrying with us and working through medicine to *restore* health, not break it. I know you as Healer, Restorer, Guide, and loving Parent.

And even though I can't seem to find you in this spot where our loved one's taking a turn for the worst, I *can* feel your presence as if it were the gentle kiss of a butterfly's wing brushing against my frightened heart.

Perhaps I can't see you because tears of grief are clogging my eyes, and rage at illness's unfairness is blinding me. I am glad you came to find me when I'd lost my way at the turn.

Hand in hand, Lord, we'll make it wherever this turn of events may lead, sharing grief, sharing hope, sharing a renewed vision of what lies ahead. Even this illness can undergo a turnaround, just like my heart.

Words to Hold You: "Thou, O Lord, be not far off . . .; hasten to my assistance. For He has not despised nor abhorred the affliction of the afflicted . . .; But when he cried to Him for help, He heard" (Psalm 22:19,24, NASB).

Pray Anyway

I don't know if you're anywhere around, Lord. And the way things are going, I can't believe you're paying attention to what's happening. I've never felt more lonely. Do you know how serious this illness is? how frightened, alone and tired I am? how distraught the family is?

Help me, us, to believe that you do. Help me to assume your presence even in the emptiness that clogs this sickroom with fear. I'm making a leap of faith here, for even though I feel you aren't attentive, I need to pray anyway.

Sometimes, Lord, when we've not been with you in awhile, we feel more comfortable at first reciting a child's prayer or a grace we once knew, or repeating a verse that Grandmother read—anything to reconnect with you. And sometimes we can best begin by talking to someone we know who is with you, yet who still feels close to us—a grandmother/grandfather, friend, mate, who can be our heavenly advocate while we search for you.

Hear me as I pray "as if" you are here with me, with us, here *for* me.

Curiously, ever-present God, I feel better. Just the *act of praying* reminded me that I am not, we are not, alone and without options. Starting to talk to you as if you care and are there revives my awareness of you. Sharing my loneliness for you brings me fresh insight into new ways I can receive your healing. It's as if I've prayed after all.

Words to Hold You: "'. . . and lo, I am with you always, even to the end of the age'" (Matthew 28:20b, NASB).

If Only

In the face of illness, two words haunt me, Lord, disturbing my rest and taxing my soul: if only. "If only" I'd lived a fuller, nicer, more faithful life or been a better friend, mate, relative, worker when I had the chance.

When trouble like illness comes, we begin many sentences and prayers with "If only." Suddenly we see opportunities we've wasted, love we've hoarded, gifts of friends and family we've squandered. O Lord, we regret many moments of our lives, ashamedly lying here now running our fingers over each one like shells collected on travels.

Help us to get rid of our regrets, for they are as toxic as illnesses invading our bodies. To live in regret is to ignore your gift of grace that says anything can be redeemed, even misspent yesterdays. We regret not having accepted it sooner! Help us to learn to move on, redo, and change.

Help us to see that regrets *can* be blessings in disguise, offering us a chance to change our lives . . . or at least our minds and our hearts.

Named like items on Saturday's shopping list, Lord, we now bring our regrets to you for healing just as we do our sick bodies. Hold our hands while we whisper our regrets, asking for forgiveness and ways to change.

We feel better getting regret out of our systems; now we can concentrate on getting well and putting our redeemed regrets into action.

Words to Hold You: ". . . forgetting what lies behind and straining forward to what lies ahead, I press on . . ." (Philippians 3:13b-14, RSV).

The Other Sufferers

"How can you be sad?" well-meaning people ask. "He's going to a better place." "She's had a good life." "You've had a long time together." "It's for the best. . . . God's will . . . buckle down, cheer up."

Like Job's friends, who may be the worst comforters in history, our friends, too, Lord, say things that don't help in these dreadful moments of illness and loss and make me feel more lonely and uncertain.

Guide them beyond handing out platitude, explanation, and prediction to a broader understanding of how to help and support; guide them to a deeper well of words . . . or sometimes to no words, for we may want them to simply sit with us and hold our hand.

Remind me, Lord, that whatever I am feeling is all right, that to cry, grieve, rage, sit numbly and dumbly or chatter incessantly—whatever I need to do to get through these moments—is very much OK. Grief is not rational, sensible, or even controllable and has a life of its own. This is good, for I believe it will take me forward if people don't interfere!

In calmer moments, Lord, I'll be grateful for the intentions of the well-meaning whose insensitive, unaware remarks make this time tougher. I even feel sorry for them, for it's as if they suffer from never having suffered. Or if they did, they didn't learn what helps, what hurts.

Teach them quickly; I need support and comfort now.

Words to Hold You: "'I have heard many such things; miserable comforters are you all. Shall windy words have an end?'" (Job 16:2-3a, RSV).

Blessed Assurance

We want to believe we can get well, Lord, but wonder if we will as we weigh statistics and consider possibilities. Where can we find evidence of assurance that you want healing and wellness for us? assurance that anything is possible, even recovery?

Where is the well from which we can draw up assurance and hope like cool water in a bucket?

All around us, you say, Lord? Where?

Help us to see it in others' healing and recovery, in those whose quality of life is not destroyed by illness, in those for whom even renegotiated life remains a source of joy. We see you in their lives; we do feel reassured.

Assurance of your life-giving power is visible in your natural creation too, Lord, where ferns unfurl through the snow; grubs become dragonflies; seeds, trees; storms, rainbows; single cells become people and animals; winter, summer; cocoons, butterflies.

We must not treat you as unfairly as we do the daisy, plucking its petals and saying, ". . . loves, me, loves me not." With you, the answer is always "loves me."

Why, then, would you, God of all nature, not create wellness and order in our beings as well? We have our answer from love all around us and can rest and heal, assured of your presence working within our bodies. They are no less than beloved parts of your marvelous re-creation.

Words to Hold You: "Cast all your anxieties on him, for he cares about you" (1 Peter 5:7, RSV).

Putting It Off

It's as angry red as a harvest sun, Lord, this mole that's kept drawing attention. For others, it's a cough, lump, change, soreness, something not quite as usual that is ice in the mind when we face it.

"How long," doctors chide when finally sought, "has it been going on?" Options are limited now, odds not good in this foolish lottery of self we've been playing.

Forgive us for our complicity in our own illness and disease. Remind us when the "Why?" question reverberates wall-to-wall that it is not a question for you, but for ourselves—the ones who wait too long; smoke, drink, and eat too much; ignore prevention and intervention measures; the ones who disregard warning signals until it's too late for simple solutions and minor procedures to fix small problems.

Why *do* we wait? Why *do* we let loose something merely worrisome in the beginning to run in roughshod boots rampant through our lives?

Why, Lord?

Nudge and empower us sooner to scurry to doctors who prefer being bothered with our worrying to our waiting, putting off.

And rather than our saying, *"Why?"* when we notice something a bit worrisome, teach us instead to say, *"Why not?"* to the idea of checking it out. A single word can make a lifetime of difference.

Words to Hold You: "'I will never fail nor forsake you'"
(Hebrews 13:5b, RSV).

Our Turn: At Our Own Hand

Creator God, we tan, smoke, and fatten our bodies as if they're indestructible machines and are so surprised, so betrayed, when the fried chickens, so to speak, come home to roost in heart attack, obesity, and laboring lungs.

We do so much to ourselves in the name of freedom and then blame you when we find ourselves falling apart at the weakened seams.

Why did you create us free? Was it poor judgment on your part? A test? Have we surprised even you with our reckless disregard of self?

We confess, even as we may secretly blame you, that we know it wasn't you who lit cigarettes, cut pies, and scooped puddings; it wasn't you who poured drinks, ignored warning symptoms, and stressed our lives away. We can see our role in this and may let you off the hook, although like children we protest, "But you shouldn't have let me!"

Be with us as we face our consequences of illness; help us to not heap on too much self-blame for we need our strength to repair and renew.

May this *interlude of illness* at our own hand be no more than that, Lord, an *interlude*, a brief moment. May it also be life-changing as we open our eyes to how wonderful life can be when we are partners with you in creative, healthful days.

Help us to achieve reunion with our bodies—not as indestructible machines to be misused, but rather as homes for your Spirit, created as we are in your image. And, really, Lord, would we treat the home of a friend the way we treat our bodies? From now on, we'll be better tenants.

Words to Hold You: "Do you not know that you are God's temple and that God's Spirit dwells in you?" (1 Corinthians 3:16, RSV).

Visiting Hours

A sick friend, Lord, leaves us feeling helpless and overwhelmed, for the gap between what *needs to be done* and what we *can do* is huge. It's easier not to visit than face inadequacies when we do. But go we must, for we want to do what we can.

Yet what I have to offer my friend is often no more than the routine of my visits to the bedside that has interrupted our time together. Is it enough, Lord? Just a visit, just regularly stopping by?

At least, we laugh, when it is Tuesday it's "my" day. Maybe routine *is* enough to anchor assumptions that people still care, people still remember and want to be involved in these days too, even if different from before. Bless our routine efforts on behalf of our friends.

Use your transforming power, Lord, to re-create into tokens of care the ordinary things we bring with us, like smells on our clothes of traffic and spring rain or of onions on our hands from chopping veggies for supper, like the punch line of a joke we retell, the scrap of news we pass on. Transform the ordinary we offer into passwords of caring, of love.

With your help, our routine—sometimes reluctant and bumbling visits created from life's ordinariness—can be a bridge from the isolated place of illness back into a wellness world that is waiting for our friends.

Words to Hold You: "The prayer offered in faith will restore the one who is sick . . ." (James 5:15, NASB).

Uplifting

Sometimes, God, we can see no farther than the ends of our noses. Like barbed-wire fences, worries erect boundaries around us and we sit, stuck. We don't want to visit the sick, for it will make us feel sad, hopeless, helpless. After all, what can we do on just a visit?

Who is the most healed when we *do* visit our sick ones? We are, lifted and inspired by just being in their presence. We're moved by their acceptance of the unacceptable and ministered to by their response to it.

They are brave enough to grieve, freeing us to. They have hope enough to persevere and dignity enough to inspire, and we are inspired. Their appreciation of our bumbling visiting calls us to learn to do it better.

Becoming comfortable with caring for and calling on our sick loved ones is a process, Lord, and we have much to learn. Help us to understand that it is not so much *what* we do or say, but that we do or say *anything*. Remind us that from our smallest efforts you can create huge amounts of loving and supporting; your presence with us on these visits redeems us all.

And in the end, once we are home, we know we have been healed a bit ourselves, healed of self-doubt, shyness, fear. We have been "lifted by love," their love of life; family; wellness; you, God; and even of us with our reluctant but now willing hands and hearts to come calling again.

Words to Hold You: "Beloved, let us love one another, for love is from God" (1 John 4:7a, NASB).

Take Something Small

We pace and wring empty hands as we search for something to fill them with. Someone we care about is ill and we want to help, but, Lord, we have little to offer.

Nothing we can think to do will make a big difference and we feel helpless and insignificant. In the face of this illness, needs are great, yet our resources are limited.

"I'm going to take a toy," a child suggests as we stew, holding a favorite plaything to take to a gravely ill friend. Long past the age of toys, the recipient of this well-used toy brightens at the gesture, healing a bit from misery, in the openhanded sharing of a child's best efforts.

Lord, send us to do likewise. Fill our empty hands with small things that simply say we care and think about them in our day-to-day lives, for we do. Send us with a pretty rock or wildflower we found on a walk that reminded us of their love of nature. Send us with a book from the library we know they enjoyed; send us to read a page or two.

Send us to feed their goldfish or tabby cat, to mow a lawn or shovel a walk as small ways to help out. Send us to walk in fund-raising events to cure their disease. Send us to . . . O Lord, our possibilities are endless!

Like children we do have special things for our hands to take to sick friends; sometimes taking just our own hands to hold theirs is enough.

Words to Hold You: "You can be sure that whoever gives even a drink of cold water . . . will certainly receive a reward" (Matthew 10:42, GNB).

Buddies

My friend is a remarkable person, Lord, a best friend. *And, what, my friend, are we going to do with our plans to grow old together?* I cry silently as I sit in my car, afraid to go to visiting hours. *It's not time; it's not time*, is all I can say. *We haven't finished being friends.*

Are you there as they thread needles into veins? Are you there wiping away misery with a cool cloth? Are you there in the sly hours just before dawn when the worst fears seem certain to come true? I would be if I could. Lord, be there for me long beyond "visiting hours."

Let memories of our movie marathons, shopping jaunts, late-night conversations, and easy pleasure in one another's company fill restless nights with peaceful dreams of anticipation, for we have much yet to do.

I'm a coward, Lord, and don't want to face this illness, especially the part that reminds of my own vulnerability. I'm uncomfortable with my own good fortune when a best friend is so ill. Please remind me that you plan healing and wholeness for both of us, *all* of us—that you didn't choose either of us to be afflicted or spared. Remind me that illness happens.

Help me most of all to focus on your promises of companionship through the dark valleys where friends cannot go. Be there in my place and remind me that I *am* being a channel for your healing power in cards I send, phone calls I make, errands I run, prayers I whisper by the bed.

When you need me to do more, send me; that's what friends are for.

Words to Hold You: *"Dear friend, I pray that you may enjoy good health and that all may go well with you . . ." (3 John 1:2, NIV).*

Keeping Time

Modern watches keep time with a silent digital hum much too easy to blend with the other sounds of today, and we don't hear the hours moving, Lord.

Until we get a wake-up call like illness.

Then we start listening as time begins ticking in a loud pocket-watch rhythm measuring the distance between *now* and *whenever*. How we wish we'd started listening earlier so we wouldn't have wasted a precious moment.

The moments—many or few—ahead of us, we won't waste, and we plan to learn line dancing, to sing in the holiday play, to canoe a new river, plant a tree, to visit relatives we've been putting off. To *sit* in the roses, never mind just smelling them!

No more, Lord, no more putting off until tomorrow, for our watch ticks time only in *todays* . . . as it always did, even if we paid little attention until now. But now is better than never.

Thank you for the gift of this new time so that we may live fully between its ticking hands. Be with us every moment so that they are lived full to running over with the richness of today—all any of us have. It is enough.

Words to Hold You: "You don't even know what your life tomorrow will be!" (James 4:14a, GNB).

Train in the Rearview Mirror

What a surprise, Lord! The diagnosis is good, my prognosis, excellent. I've been granted a reprieve. How high do I dare jump in the hospital hall? How loud do I dare shout, *"Hallelujah!"* as I run into the parking lot?

Thank you for this chance . . . this second chance. Forgive me for being surprised as if healing were beyond possibility and your intention.

I am learning other lessons from this illness too, Lord, so important that I feel like writing them as a child would on a school tablet. That's how new I feel, like a kid on the first day at school, for I'd feared it was to be my last.

I'm learning that it's scary to drive across railroad tracks in the country, only to look up and see a train in the rearview mirror. That's what this illness is for me: a train in the rearview mirror.

I am fortunate—blessed—to be alive. May I be smart enough to think seriously about how to stay that way! How easy it would be to slip back into old ways that misuse my body and encourage illness.

Put my hand on the tracks of memory so I can feel vibrations of a train. With your grace and my attentiveness, may it be vibrations of this illness *behind* me and not an impending collision for someone holding a second chance who doesn't have gratitude enough to get out of the way!

During my daily prayers, remind me to add, *"Please, Lord, teach me to laugh again, but don't ever let me forget that I cried."* Wise me up, Lord.

Words to Hold You: "I sought the LORD, and he answered me, and delivered me from all my fears" (Psalm 34:4, RSV).

Minor Complaints

The doctor says it's not serious, Lord. If I felt better, I'd be properly grateful, but I still feel miserable. I don't know what I'd do if I really got sick since a cold or flu reduces me to a limp, whimpering dishrag!

But really it's mostly garden-variety ailments that fill our medicine cabinets with more remedies than you can shake a thermometer at. We devour symptoms of new diseases with a fervor only matched when reading of new cures. We worry ourselves into illness!

"Rest, keep warm, and drink plenty of fluids," was advice good enough for our ancestors, but catch us waiting out any mild ailment; we want to be well *right now*. Is impatience a treatable malady, Lord? Is whining fear a preventable condition?

These minor ailments, however, do keep us humble, reminding us we can go to the moon and across the world in the punch of a jet ticket but can't cure the common cold or hurry up the old-fashioned flu.

We secretly love it: *old-fashioned flu*. It conjures up images of long-ago mentholated chest rubs, cool Mother-hands on hot foreheads, soup served on a tray in bed, homework dropped off by a friend, naps with the cat asleep on our quilt-covered knees. It was a pleasure to get well.

Slow us down and prescribe couch convalescence for our depleted bodies, easy prey to hardier, more serious germs. There's just something about a cup of tea, Lord—when we *take time* to sip it with you—that heals more than minor sore throats.

***Words to Hold You:** "Your recovery will speedily spring forth . . ." (Isaiah 58:8b, NASB).*

Life in Our Own Hands

We've just had a bad scare, Lord: the heart beat unevenly; a lump slipped beneath our fingers; a cough didn't go away; a sore didn't heal.

We had them checked out. There's no problem, nothing to worry about.

Remind us, Lord, when we forget, that we hold life in our own hands in trust from you. Thank you for these harmless reminders that keep us on our toes. Steady our hands as we dial for appointments at the first sign of trouble. Nudge us to *check it out, check it out* as any parent would nudge a child to do.

Thank you for glimpses of life ahead that come in our terror-filled speculations. It helps to envision the joy you have in store for us when we consider putting off, taking chances with our futures because we're afraid.

Diligent self-care is a small price to pay for a full ride toward those days of the rest of our lives, Lord, regardless of what we encounter. Keep us vigilant and brave enough to pursue worries; reassure us that most of the time what we find may be just an interruption, a temporary roadblock.

Send us for routine checkups near our birthdays, easy dates to remember. And when we come home we'll toss a prayer aloft to your waiting hands: "Many happy returns of my day. May there be many more."

Words to Hold You: "We know that in everything God works for good . . ." (Romans 8:28a, RSV).

The Missing Piece

Half of me is missing, God, for this dear mate of mine is ill. Actually, *more* than half of me feels missing, for much of who I am is intricately connected and mutually experienced.

I am torn between praying for this dearest one and for myself, for we both need prayer under the onslaught of illness: one of us for health, the other—me—for strength, courage, and stamina enough for two!

Restore full measures of health. Bring comfort during the fearful times, and dull the aches and pains. Guide and inspire the nurses and doctors as you and they work together for healing. Use me where you can, for I would give my life to "make it all better," as we laugh when we can.

And, God, please remember me and "make it all better" for me too while illness is separating us in lonely nights where there are no feet to link with in an empty bed, no "Good nights" to sigh in sleepy unison, when there are decisions that two heads make better than one.

Restore us to being a "twosome" soon, and remind us when recovery is complete to remember this interval as a wake-up call for savoring times together. Thank you for being the linking hand between our two missing halves, making us whole despite the intrusion of illness.

Words to Hold You: "Two are better off than one. . . . If one of them falls down, the other can help him up. . . . If it is cold, two can sleep together and stay warm. . . ." (Ecclesiastes 4:9-11, GNB).

I Still Do

Lord, the vows we took to love and cherish ". . . in sickness and in health" were made without any suspicion there would be days like these. Had I known then what I do now as I stand beside this sickbed, I confess the words "I do" might have stuck crossways in my throat.

From my knees I also confess I am sometimes nearly ready to retract those vows, for I don't know how much more illness I can take. I don't know how much more fear, pain, and misery I can bear, how many more sights, smells, and moods I can endure.

I confess I am sometimes a "fair-weather" mate, and cringe beneath my weakness. Help me to be strong; hold me as I breathe in, breathe out, in, out, to gain a second wind for this chapter of our life together. Remind me that it shall pass and become like a ring on a tree that tells our tale.

Do I still love as I did when first inspired to say, "I do?" Oh, yes, Lord, and more, for time has enriched us, a resource to draw upon now. Help me to *be* a resource and reservoir of strength for my mate's use.

Side by side in our minds as we hold hands, we are snuggled together even in this maze of tubes and gadgets. No matter how rough this or any illness may be, with your hand leading us through it, I vow to love *even* in sickness, knowing you can help us redeem it into opportunity to grow still closer.

Help me, Lord, as *I do.*

Words to Hold You: "Love never gives up; and its faith, hope, and patience never fail" (1 Corinthians 13:7, GNB).

Rungs of a Ladder: Stages of Grief

Like verses in the song "Jacob's Ladder" we, too, are climbing a ladder, the ladder of grief: denial, anger, bargaining, depression, acceptance. It sounds so simple, doesn't it, Lord? It sounds so easy to run up the ladder—one, two, three, four, five.

Except few things, especially grief, are as neat and tidy as that, and few journeys unfold free of detours, stalls, and roadblocks. Illness provides plenty of them.

Help us to move from rung to rung, up and down, here and there as often as we need, for strength is gained from each one as it leads us to the best: acceptance. It is there we will find ease from the other ones.

Acceptance is not to give up, Lord. To the contrary, it is to accept *what is* and then move on to *what can be*, fortified and peacefully strong. With your healing power, that can be so many wonderful things.

Climbing back and forth, back and forth from one rung on grief's ladder to another, we will move through each place of understanding and coping, no matter the diagnosis or prognosis. And even when it is good we grieve, for we've lost the belief that illness is what happens to other folks, not to us and ours.

We are grateful that this ladder is a flexible and sturdy one, Lord, for we will be climbing around on it to make sense of our grief, knowing that each step will eventually make a complete journey.

Words to Hold You: "'I will never leave you nor forsake you'" (Hebrews 13:5b, NKJV).

Flow Like a River

Where else are there so many unshed tears than in the midst of illness? these worrying waiting rooms? these cubicles of pain and anguish?

"Be strong." "Buck up." "Chin up." "Stiff upper lip." "Put on a brave face." "Hush crying." "Tough it out."

They say it all, Lord, the well-intentioned who think your only gift for bearing troubles and enduring grief is stoic, bucked-up silence.

Yet we remember that you've given us the greater gift of tears, those healing streams that cleanse the soul. Their impulsive overflowing comes from our deeply stoppered hurts and fears. Thank you, Lord, for their refreshing hiccups of release.

How wise and benevolent you are to provide tears to heal both our spirits and bodies, both your habitations. Even scientists remind us that tears are useful: tears from joy are mere H_2O, and tears from peeling onions are mostly salty water when pondered beneath their microscopes.

However, tears from grief and sadness are made of toxins flushed from deep within our pain. If left stoppered by stiff upper lips and brave faces they pollute our very beings. Their release, though, reminds us of your promise that comfort comes to those who have courage to mourn.

Thank you for wet cheeks; red, swollen eyes; and runny noses. They are evidence of your wise, comforting presence.

Words to Hold You: "Those who mourn are fortunate! for they shall be comforted" (Matthew 5:4, TLB).

Rock-a-Bye, Baby

How quickly our wee ones can get sick, Lord. In the blink of an eye, a turn of the head, these babies are burning with fever and shaking with symptoms they can't tell us about except in a wail!

How helpless we feel trying to interpret. How helpless we feel when overshadowed by the technology sometimes needed to heal them. How useless we feel too, for we weren't able to protect them from illness' alarms.

Be with them in their insulated nursery nests and the high, sterile cribs that dwarf their sweet smiles and usually busy bodies. Help us to not overreact so that when they get well we'll let them be bumbling and bustling as babies must be. Calm our fears even as you keep us gently vigilant; there's no need for further alarm.

Be with us now as we rock and lullaby these little ones; sing along with us new words of assurance and comfort. Be with us as we kneel beside their cribs and Isolettes, croup tents, bassinets, and gently gather them up in prayer to lay in your hands. We gently whisper that it is you holding them, Lord, so they can speak with you too, in the joyous, babbling baby talk that delights you as it does us.

As we climb to our feet, Lord, we are comforted even in our concern, for we can see the imprint of your hand on the baby brow and know you are here, sitting up close beside the bed.

Words to Hold You: "'. . . so will I seek out my sheep. . . . and I will bind up the crippled, and I will strengthen the weak . . .'" (Ezekiel 34:12-16, RSV).

Love's Lullaby

Kids lie so unnaturally quiet, Lord, in sickbeds where freckles and suntans, skinned knees and snaggletoothed grins seem out of place. Illness has come like a thief in the night and stolen the innocence of their childhoods and broken our hearts. Underlying our fears we are angry on behalf of them, for being cheated of carefree play days. May it not be life; oh, please, Lord, not life.

Even as we worry, we marvel at how you wisely created children so resilient, and we are humbled at how they can cope! From one minute to the next, they're both stoic patients *and* rowdy rascals despite IVs, casts, and limitations. They make us laugh and they make us cry as they cope better than we do! Lighten us up to match their spirits.

Urge us to respect their intelligence and tell them the truth about the illness that has sidelined them from play, for in their wise ways they already know what we're not saying. Remind us to enlist them in their own care, for they have the energy of the young, plus claim a close place beside your knee, Lord, from which to draw strength.

Be here should they call out in nighttime frights and fever's alarm. Stay close to us too, for we have aching, empty arms longing to hold them and make them well. Together, let's hum a lullaby of healing, our duet of love serving as a night-light for even the darkest children's hour.

Words to Hold You: "Fear not, for I am with you, be not dismayed . . .; I will strengthen you . . ." (Isaiah 41:10, RSV).

Room on a Lap

We would hold our children on a lap if we could, Lord, but their feet dangle and their heads miss the shoulder mark. Our grownup children are sick, and we don't know how to tend them.

Illness packs a wallop when it hits these special people—as they've become instead of being "our children"—for they've just begun to reap life's rewards. Be with them as they face this as valiantly as they used to face dragons beneath beds. Arm them with recollected youthful vigor and childlike trust in you and in us to keep dragons at bay.

Guide us as parents, grandparents, for we are tempted to rush in and slay the dragons for them—and we would if we could. We'll be their best "cheerleaders," for we want them to know they have the strength and resources to slay those nasty dragons; we're just back-up.

Be with us late at night when we remove our brave parental faces—you know, the ones we've worn all their lives, Lord, so they won't know how scared we are of the for-real dragons of illness, accident, and trauma that prowl in the night. Hold our hands while we worry and rage, for it isn't fair they've come through childhood only to have devastating illness overtake them now. Spare them any scars worse than chicken pox!

And, Lord, make a lap big enough to hold both parent and grown-up child. We both need to be comforted from the night-time terrors of illness. This time the dragon is real. Help us to send it packing.

Words to Hold You: "'. . .how often I have longed to gather your children together, as a hen gathers her chicks under her wings . . .'" (Matthew 23:37, NIV).

Let's Run a Few Tests

Lord, these marvels of *modern technology*, which can so precisely show and tell, are a mixed blessing. We cower before the wizardry of the wavy lines, the black-and-white negatives as the doctors squint, study, evaluate, decide.

There's no hiding from the rays and beams that search into each crevice and cranny for intruders, and we are as terrified of the process as of its findings. And the waiting is even worse, for we fear it is just the first of many waiting moments in store for us.

Be with us as we shiver flimsy-gowned and alone on this side of the diagnosis. It's not really the routines or the gowns; it's the parentheses we suddenly find ourselves between: life and death. We've been there all along, but we just noticed today as we wait to find out what will be doled out to us by unblinking machines.

While we are waiting, Lord, cradle us as the wailing, lost children we've become. Help us to hold fast to dignity even as fear wrestles it away like a paper gown torn from our backs. Assure us of your presence, no matter the bottom line being tallied up behind lead screens and computer consoles.

O Lord, take our hands while we wait; we're so cold.

Words to Hold You: "Let him have all your worries and cares, for he is always thinking about you and watching everything that concerns you" (1 Peter 5:7, TLB).

Uneasy Chairs

Waiting rooms, Lord, are great levelers. Time spent in them feels the same for all of us—rich or poor, young or old—for dread and worry are the same. The clocks seem slower, air thicker, lights dimmer, no matter who we are outside the waiting-room doors.

Separated from our everyday props of house, yard, bank account, and job, we who hunch together at opposite ends of stiff, unibody-shaped furniture become members of the same club: The Ones Left Behind.

No matter if for some of our loved ones the procedures are "routine." Let's face it, routine is what is done to someone else, not me or mine!

And for some of us, Lord, grief and terror have themselves become routine as we wait for even a small bit of good news to rise from the ashes of the bad news we've been enduring.

No matter the range of reasons that we are here, we admit to being more than a little worried, our hands clutching one another as if hunting for the loved ones' hands we usually hold. Beyond the swinging doors, they are blissfully unaware of our concern; be with them.

And as the minutes become hours, hold each of us by the hand, Lord, and pour your healing power from us to them. Transform our fears into energized, active prayers, into trust in the process of healing and recovery. Scoot us over on these uncomfortable couches to make room for you; we need a companion for the waiting.

Words to Hold You: "We put our hope in the LORD; he is our protector and our help" (Psalm 33:20, GNB).

Striking a Bargain

Let's bargain, Lord: what can we promise, give up, give away that will persuade you to grant us more life? We will do anything, be anybody if you will wake us up now, reassuring us that this illness is just a bad dream.

As we wait for test results, we're praying Jesus' prayer, ". . . let this cup pass from me," and it's easy to understand his anguish. "Let this one pass from me and I'll be a new person . . . better, kinder, giving, and loving *if* you'll wipe away any blemish from my tests," we bargain.

Is that you, Lord, bringing us a calming moment? Have you come to bargain? or simply to be nearby in this waiting place as you were with him in the garden?

Now, with you here, we find the strength to whisper the rest of his prayer, ". . . *if it be your will*, let this cup pass from me." Your will, Lord, not ours, no matter what we would bargain in exchange. Your will, no matter how difficult for us to trust it.

Yet your will for healing and wholeness is always your end of the bargain, and we may yet be spared a bitter cup . . . or not. Either way, we will live fully as the new people we've promised you we will be; that's our end of a new bargain.

We are grateful for the comfort in having you close enough by to hear our dread, our hope, our bargaining prayers to be spared.

Words to Hold You: "I will lie down in peace and sleep, for . . . you will keep me safe" (Psalm 4:8, TLB).

Urgent! Send Cures
(dedicated to Nancy, who's hurrying)

So many diseases, so little time, Lord. And we wait in equal parts of hope and heart-pounding anxiety for cures and preventatives to reach us before it's too late. Thank you for those who hurry to get them to us.

We jump at the first sound of a new pill in a bottle, a new potion to swallow, a new clinical trial to join, for life is so precious we don't want to lose a single minute. Thank you for those who work overtime so we won't.

Speed up the inventors still faster; progress feels as if it moves at the pace of chilled molasses. Fill dreamers of cures with visions and formulas in their microscopic worlds. Guide their hands in tasks that seem to us to take forever.

Yet for many there is no forever . . . hardly even a tomorrow, and we are chanting, *"Now, now, now."* Topple political and financial roadblocks that keep us and science waiting for the sake of money and power; unclog a system that withholds healing for the sake of the bottom line.

And for those whose discoveries can free us from illness, sustain their eyesight and ease their necks and backs that protest long hours and cramped positions spent over test tubes and our great need.

Give them clues, Lord, for getting on the right track. Speed up their research while you slow-motion disease. There is no luxury of time in the race to a finish line no one wants to cross.

Words to Hold You: "We live by faith, not by sight" (2 Corinthians 5:7, NIV).

Aliens

The gap is no bigger than a word, Lord—*diagnosis*—yet it plunges us into an eternal chasm of alienation. As soon as it is uttered, our world divides itself into *us* and *them*. We feel alienated from family, friends, and everyone else who is well while we are sick. It's as if we speak foreign languages, as if we now wear alien skins.

How can other people go on as if nothing is changed? Now that ours has lost it, life's normalcy is maddening as routine goes around us like a stream around rocks.

We want our illness not to be true, yet it's our only focus. We resent those with the luxury of divided attention. We used to be like them, caring if the baseball season continues, if it rains or snows, who wins elections, and how much weight to lose! Foreign languages.

Hold us, Lord, for not many people like to touch aliens. We hunger for hands to hold, a shoulder to lean on, feeling unused in body and soul as we shrivel from the absence of touch, the first sign we had that we are alien.

We gratefully know we are not alien to you. Come speak this new language with us so we'll never be alone, different, outcast even by our own moods and worries, by our symptoms and limits. No, we're not alien, Lord, we're still your children, included forever in your circle of love.

Words to Hold You: "Keep me as the apple of your eye" (Psalm 17:8a, NIV).

"A" Is for AIDS

Today's alphabet begins with "A" for AIDS, Lord, and we gather in a grieving circle around those afflicted with this terrible, wasting disease.

We confess we are afraid of the disease, of the diseased, of getting diseased. We are only slowly learning to tend, to care. We would be different if we could, but we can't seem to rid ourselves of the plague of fear, secrecy, and shame. It leaves us as good as dead when hands are used only for pointing in angry, shaming fingers or wringing in despair.

But these sufferers are our children, friends, mates, peers, parents, grandchildren, neighbors. These sufferers are us, Lord; be near. Restrain any from using this illness as a weapon to beat others into submission. Cleanse wild imaginations of time-consuming accusations and refill them with plans of action, of education, of prevention and cures. Remind us we are called to serve and heal in your name, not to judge.

Comfort those who are doubly hurt when the disease of fear, secrecy, and shame compound their illness; they have enough to endure. Comfort those who watch and wait, keeping life/death vigils beside loved ones who come in all sizes, ages, and colors.

Shake us into sensibility so that we pull our heads from the sands of wishful thinking, proclamation, and denunciation and get on with what life-saving efforts we can.

Today's alphabet begins with "A," Lord, for acceptance, assistance.

Words to Hold You: "For the LORD has comforted His people, And will have compassion on His afflicted" (Isaiah 49:13b, NASB).

Wounded Souls, Broken Spirits
(dedicated to J. R. Hayes, M.D.)

There are seventeen cracks in the celery-green couch where she waits. The doctor is on schedule, *Thursday, 4:30 p.m.*; time to retrieve her soul, God of all last things.

Go with her, God, and all who endure illness of mind and spirit as they move from its darkness into the healing light of conversation, of therapy.

There's no cause for shame, but many "in therapy" are uncomfortable, as if tattered underwear is showing. When we stammer, remind us of your son, who cast out all the demons he could find. We have fancier names for our inner ailments these days, but they still possess and bind.

Remind us, too, that it takes great courage to heal, great courage to touch the hem of your garment and ask for healing. Bless the brave voices telling nightmare tales to gifted healers into whose lap they crawl carrying their dreadful wounds. Together they are retrieving and binding up damaged parts and laying down burdens carried so long.

Who doesn't know at least moments of mind darkness, the lure of its seductive stagnation? Rescue those for whom moments become months, become years, become lives. Retrieve and restore them.

Bless the mind-and-soul healers who pursue lost wanderers down tunnels of despair. Endow them with energy, humor, and skill for the chase. Give them incredible patience as they wrestle with the hurting ones, like dogs scrapping over a bone in the yard, tugging and pulling at the truth you promise will set everyone free.

God of understanding, bless the hard work of therapy, where we need only reach out a hand and feel the hem of your robe to know we're not alone in our efforts.

Words to Hold You: "Be renewed in the spirit of your minds, and put on the new nature . . ." (Ephesians 4:23-24, RSV).

Skin Deep

Some illnesses, treatments, and surgeries mutilate and disfigure us, twisting us into caricatures. We turn away from everyone in shame as oddballs, grotesque freaks; we turn away, Lord, even from you.

Forgive our rage at you when we look in a mirror at our own marred reflection. Forgive our fury when we look at a loved one now tucked into a not-pretty skin or into an illness-contorted body.

Help us to believe you want wholeness for us all, Lord, on the outside as well as inside. Help us to know we *are* whole, capable, and beloved children, despite blemished, misshapen, mismatched bodies.

Be with us when we must endure strangers' rude stares and remarks. Stand with us beneath pointing fingers. Be with us as we testify of your love by not hating the pointers, the gigglers.

Give us words and explanations to generously offer so others will be reminded when they get to know us that beauty is truly only skin deep.

Keep us lovely on the inside, Lord, while you help us to become lovely on the outside if that is to be; if not, help us to feel lovely anyhow, for we are.

Words to Hold You: "For as he thinketh in his heart, so is he" (Proverbs 23:7a, KJV).

Tag-a-Longs

We drag our oxygen tanks, walkers, canes, catheters, and monitors around with us, Lord, like children with pull toys. We are never going to get better, and only hope to stay even with this chronic disease.

This is not how we anticipated our futures, tethered to machines and restrained between the limits enforced by illness. We move up and down the ladder of grief, for we still can't believe this is happening to us. We still cry, "Why?" We still look too far down the road even though we can't see beyond our immediate limits.

Raise our sights and help us to adapt, to be creative in ways to get around, get by, get along. Help us to not stay stuck in ruts of grief; ease it, Lord, for we want to move as far and fast as we can.

Be with our families, for theirs is a heavy load. Bless friends who accept us as we are . . . and may become. Bless our special caregivers; together they are all picking up the pieces of our lives that we're losing.

We are grateful for good days when body, mind, and soul cooperate. We begrudge the time and energy that rough days drain from us; help us to navigate around them like rocks in a stream we *can* move beyond.

Help us also to be chronically hopeful, Lord, as if we are tugging around balloons of your love and care along with the apparatus needed in everyday living. Every day—is there any other way to live? Keep us mindful of that when we worry too much about the future. Every day we will come to you for encouragement, support.

Words to Hold You: ". . . you have always cared for me in my distress; now hear me as I call again" (Psalm 4:1a, TLB).

Interpreter

Be our interpreter, Lord, for this debilitating illness tangles words and movement into mismatched, halting efforts that we yearn to turn into conversation and companionship with loved ones who are laid low by strokes of misfortune.

Pain is on both sides of these efforts, for there are still places to go, words to say. Help us to find ways to communicate *what* and then give us the creativity to figure out *where* and *how*.

You who made crooked paths straight and mountains low can surely make crooked smiles straight again, make halting limbs leap. We pray this first, Lord. But we cling to your promise of comfort and companionship if it is not to be; help us all to live in this new place of limitation. Strengthen us—caregivers, mates, family, friends—who tend these ailing bodies that refuse their owners' bidding; work through our efforts.

It is sometimes difficult to remember how our loved ones were before they became trapped inside the shell of illness. Let us remember them together, Lord, taking comfort in what was; it will give us strength to build on now.

Help halting hands and hesitant voices to find something important to do while waiting for lost parts to catch up. Give us patience to support and encourage, remembering that hard work begets recovery.

Be our interpreter of love that fits any language.

Words to Hold You: "Thou hast been my help. . . . My soul clings to thee; thy right hand upholds me" (Psalm 63:7-8, RSV).

No Turning Away

Illness is not pretty, Lord, and we are embarrassed by the dirty tricks our bodies can play on us. They can smell; make noises; pooch; pucker; shrivel; change color, shape, texture, and size. They can ignore manners and our intentions and embarrass us to tears.

We wear wigs, makeup, false parts, and fake smiles to hide what illness has done to us. We turn away from our loved ones, our mirrored reflections, and even from you.

We are no longer perfect, Lord, and feel diminished.

Help us learn to relove our illness-touched bodies and look without scorn and shame on wounds and modifications, for they are battle ribbons and medals of valor showing us courageous, determined, and brave in a quest for wellness.

Help us to pity others who may turn away in embarrassment or dismay, for they miss the point that we are more than the sum of all our mismatched parts! We are your beautiful children.

Bless our ostomies, wigs, makeup, grafts, implants, added parts, taken-away parts, pins, plates, rods, bolts, patches, and gadgets, for they enable us to live fully, if newly. Bless and touch our new bodies, healing our embarrassment and shame with your gentle, admiring touch.

Thank you most of all, dear Lord, for being the first not to turn away. We feel beautiful in your sight.

Words to Hold You: "For he has not despised or abhorred the affliction of the afflicted; and he has not hid his face from him, but has heard, when he cried to him" (Psalm 22:24, RSV).

Not Quite OK

The tests are completed, Lord, as if we needed results before we tally up our grief: the baby is not quite OK and never will be. Illnesses of limits come as syndrome, condition, and unpronounceable malady and break our hearts no matter how they're spelled or what their cause.

"Why?" we wail even as we are planning how to go on, how to adjust.

Guide these little ones past limits, Lord. Guide us to help. Place your gentle hands over the eyes of our hearts so we can't look too far down roads we can travel best a step at a time. Give us energy to be advocates en route.

Too long tucked away into society's dark corners, our special ones need to be brought to the front seats of life's happiest events, where their efforts can inspire us all. Give us the courage to do it. Reprimand and educate any who withhold smiles and compassion. Remind *us* to smile.

Send a special comfort to families and friends of those so profoundly locked in impairment they would not know a smile should it be offered. Guide science so that all children will be born whole enough for smiles.

Give us all hearts from which to grow smiles for special, not-quite-OK ones, Lord. We want unlimited smiles to be their companions for life.

Words to Hold You: "'Whoever receives one child like this in My name receives Me; and whoever receives Me does not receive Me, but Him who sent Me'" (Mark 9:37, NASB).

Catching Up, Slowing Down

We don't *walk* through the valley of the shadow of death, Lord; we run pell-mell as we do in almost everything until the day we are more *there* than *here*. We run until we hear those terrifying words: heart attack, disease of the heart.

We break our hearts, Lord, by living too fast but walking too slow, eating too much but avoiding what's best, worrying too often but talking too seldom, by enjoying chemicals and toxins but ignoring the results.

Thank you for paramedics, often first to pull us back. We're shocked to get the message behind the *whoop, whoop, whoop* of a life-saving siren that we'd best be changing; help us to listen for your calming presence between its wails. Thank you for guiding medical teams that keep us from crossing life's finishing line; winning is losing in this race, Lord.

We will take this gift of new life to heart, treadling bikes and walking miles at a pace more in keeping with living, not dying, which is the course we have been following.

Thank you for heart-stopping glimpses of our mortality when we arrived too soon at the pearly gates. We won't be back until it's time.

Words to Hold You: "Teach us to number our days that we may get a heart of wisdom" (Psalm 90:12, RSV).

Traveling Companions

She found her mother down on the floor, Lord, feet propped undignified on a chair, hands behind her head. Where she thought she was and what she was doing, no one had any idea, but she was laughing as if at a remembered party, in a moment of childhood play.

"Is everything better down there, Mother?" she asked from the doorway, saddened at the specter of a once-dignified woman dragged to her knees and beyond by this disease.

It addles the brain and tests the faith of those who watch from doorways, bedsides, and beyond locked wards as well as the ones playing tug-of-war with it in efforts to keep at least something of who they once were.

As we think about this mother and all parents, spouses, or ourselves sprawled out on a nursing home floor, we recall what you did so long ago in a dusty manger. You came then, Emmanuel, to keep company with all of us in our lostness, even if not as severe and embarrassing as this mother's.

And in that kind of moment, stepping out of her shoes, the daughter joined her mother on the floor, feeling your presence too, as once again you show that the best way to comfort is to be a companion in the lostness. Give us courage, stamina, and vision to do likewise.

Stay near, Lord. The view from our spot on the floor is bleak.

Words to Hold You: "He gives power to the tired and worn out, and strength to the weak" (Isaiah 40:29, TLB).

Thief in the Night

They locked doors faithfully, sliding dead bolts and hooking chains against intruders, but a thief in the night sneaked in anyhow: Alzheimer's, Lord, the disease with no cure, no hope for reprieve in the sting of a needle, the swallow of elixirs, the shuffling progress of therapy. Nothing can be done.

A thickening in the brain is clogging life like hair in a drain, and there is nothing to do but watch helplessly as wit and insight flow swiftly out of sight down the sluggish whirlpool.

They saved for old age, Lord, plunking pennies in a pink pig so they would be secure. The cost for security now can't be measured in piggy banks, for it now means hiding car keys, locking doors, unplugging appliances.

We've no security either, as we wring hands around them in a safety circle. How sad that they live their own death through a distorted filter, like salad oil on a glass, and we sob like the lost children we've all become.

Visit left-behind mates, Lord, as they lose lovers cherished for lifetimes. Hold them closely as they wail into nights they can no longer share except by the glow of a night-light beside a high-railed single bed.

Comfort the sufferers and feed them your sleeping draught of peace so restraints can be unbuckled. Add your hand to the circle of loving, fearful family members so we may rest, knowing you're vigilant in our stead.

Lead us to a cure, a preventative for this funeral with no end.

For now, send the caregivers out for a meal or movie with permission to tarry awhile in the neon-lit land of the living. There are more than enough eternal nights ahead in this crevice between life and death.

Words to Hold You: "He has sent me to bind up the brokenhearted, To proclaim liberty to captives . . ." (Isaiah 61:1b, NASB).

Sandwich Generation—A Bitter Taste

He's worked hard to get well and thinks he's coming home. He got up early, packed his suitcase, and told roommate and nurses good-bye. "Thank you for the care," he added so politely. "Won't be needing you anymore, for I'm going home."

But not with me or any of the family, Lord, and we tremble in fear that telling our special loved one will kill him, breaking fragile, patched-up heart and hopes. Or maybe it will kill us, for who can easily survive the guilt from putting one person's life ahead of another's?

But few of us are home, for we work and run hither and yon, and there's no one who can take care of wobbly, needy bodies. No one should be left alone all day, even for the sake of being "home."

Comfort us when we would take loved ones home with us if we could, but simply can't. Forgive us for being too busy, too selfish, too afraid to do it when we could but won't. Help us to know the difference.

And please be with us when we tell them they're going to a nursing home. Hint at some words we might use to soften the blow. Arm them with a dignity to bear the news so at least they retain that. Don't let them beg, Lord; that would scar us all.

I beg from my knees: take me with you before this happens to me.

Words to Hold You: "All those who know your mercy, Lord, will count on you for help" (Psalm 9:10a, TLB).

Laid Low by Alzheimer's

I can see you better from down here, Lord, as I play on the floor like the child this disease is making me. What is happening? Why am I reversing my life? What am I doing on this floor? Who are those people in the doorway? Why are they crying?

Some days I know I am doing strange things: undressing, dressing; hiding forks in my sock drawer; missing the bedroom I've walked past a dozen times; not knowing my name, which I've always thought was special. On those days, Lord, I am lost even from myself, whoever that used to be.

On other days, though, I am fine, tending a garden, making a meal, dressing in attractive clothes with manners and mind to match.

Yet this is when I worry, chasing after the vague, elusive symptoms from those other days like a child playing tag. I can't seem to control what I'll do next or know when I'll stray from myself again, getting lost on the dead-end road that is Alzheimer's. On some days, I can even spell it.

Today I am crawling on the floor, not able to understand why this makes other people cry. Send them down here to join me, to join *us*, for even on my most dim and worrisome days I recognize you and feel your hand. Forgive my manners if I forget your name; even if I don't have the right words, Lord, in my heart I call you *companion* and *friend*.

Stay here with me on good days and bad and the precarious ones in between; I feel so alone, separated as I am even from myself.

Words to Hold You: "Be not far from me, for trouble is near and there is none to help" (Psalm 22:11, RSV).

Lie Down in Green Pastures

With the tune of "Baa, Baa Black Sheep" humming in my head I willingly accept the chemo dripping into veins that both welcome and resist its potent healing.

I need you as a shepherd to tend me, Lord, settling me beside still waters that bathe my healthy cells like rain on grassy slopes. There nimble-footed sheep, like the amazing chemicals of chemo, are grazing it clean of overgrown, unruly weeds like this cancer that has crept over the fences of wellness.

Anoint my body with soothing salves as the shepherd does the sheep's when it is snagged by a bramble, for that is how I feel—snagged and scratched. Lead me to drink from clear streams of hope if nausea intrudes, as a sheep would sip from crystal creeks.

And, Lord of all nature, should I become lost in cancer's maze of unfamiliar hills and valleys, remind me that you will come and find me, never leaving me to endure the barren, dark, and scary pits alone, never allowing me to fall over the cliffs of despair.

I feel your presence in the blanket on my bed and am clinging to it like to your rough-sewn robe. As I smell the pungent odor of grazing sheep behind the antiseptic smells, I feel safe and warmed as if I am running my hands through their oily wool; it feels like gloves on a wintry day, and I am comforted, reassured.

I know you will continue to restore me as I move through treatment to the safe meadow of wellness. When I squint, Lord, I already see it.

Words to Hold You: "The Lord is my shepherd . . ."
(Psalm 23:1, NASB).

Noble Suffering?

So much suffering, Lord, is done in your name. Yet how can it be your will that we writhe in pain and howl in terror at the hands of illness? How can it be best for us, your children, to feel forsaken and condemned? Where are you in our suffering? Is it your design, your purpose in creating us?

When we look through eyes of faith, we do see suffering everywhere because it is part of your natural order, not a personal torture just for us. With eyes of faith and ears filled with grace, we can understand that you who created this natural world will not abandon it to the whim of chaos any more than you will abandon us to the whims of suffering.

Where are you in this suffering? You are everywhere, Lord, tending us when we suffer. You are in the back rub, the morphine patch, the doctor and nurses' hands. You are in the steadfast love of family and friends, in the support groups and volunteers who come to call and invite. You are in the peace that can come to our souls when we relax and let you draw near as friend and comforter, not author of our suffering.

Yet sometimes we may need to find reasons for suffering and can only find comfort in thinking it must be your will. When we no longer gain comfort believing this, Lord, help us to move on. Redeem our suffering and blame of you into knowing you instead as reliable companion, comforter.

Words to Hold You: "'Why do I keep suffering? . . . Do you intend to disappoint me like a stream that goes dry in the summer?' . . . To this the LORD replied, '. . . I will be with you . . .'" (Jeremiah 15:18-20, GNB).

X Marks the Spot

Searing like many suns, radiation beams are seeking and destroying the illness that would steal my life. I am both awed at its power and grateful for its hope. Stay near as the beams do their work, Lord, for despite the warmth of treatment, the chill of illness is here too.

Help me feel as if your summer sun is in this room, where many sunbeams form a single healing shaft of wellness to follow the map tracings on my body.

I am secure in the knowledge that light puts out darkness, Lord, even the darkness of runaway cells. And this powerful, radiating light reminds me that no darkness is bleak enough to hide you; there is always light. And where there is your light, there is the warmth of love I can feel now.

I feel it through my caregivers, my family, my friends. I feel it through the calm that comes from doing all I can to regain health. I feel it through renewed energy to choose treatments and options and to recover quickly. I am absolutely certain you are the sender of this light, Lord.

Later, as I doze to let this light continue its work, I'll open myself to your restorative sleep, another gift of your hands tending me while I heal.

Words to Hold You: "The light shines in the darkness, and the darkness has not overcome it" (John 1:5, RSV).

It Hurts

I hurt very, very badly, Lord. There are so many ways to suffer and be miserable, and I am feeling all of them.

Comfort me and help me to rest in the midst of this firestorm of pain. What can I do to stop it? to keep it from coming back? Pain robs my sleep, diminishes my strength, and changes my moods so dramatically I hardly recognize myself.

Ease my pain, Lord.

As I lay back on my pillow, turn down the volume on pain's intensity. Dilute it like mud washing away on a windshield so it can't cover my view beyond these painful days. While I doze, ease my body into a slumbering position, for I will be more comfortable that way rather than poised like a body-fist clenched to fight. Help me to relax and feel the pain go.

Thank you for pain medication, for it is a resource from you that will aid in my healing; I know there's nothing noble about grinning and bearing it. Hold me when I cry, Lord; let my tears release toxins that keep me sick. Send others to hold me too.

Remind me that this pain is temporary and can be relieved, just like my worries about it. *Needless* pain is too much to bear.

Words to Hold You: "Turn to me and be gracious to me, For I am lonely and afflicted. . . . I take refuge in Thee" (Psalm 25:16-20, NASB).

Ungrateful

I'd like to toss the lunch tray onto the rumpled bed, Lord, since there is apparently nothing good on it. The bed's disarray surely must come from within the soul, for no one as bitter and ungrateful as our loved one could be contented in a neat bed. I'm sorry I came to visit.

A soul in disarray is often ripe for a second chance, yet this special loved one appears intent upon missing it, for, surprising even the doctors, illness is responding to treatment. Yet we confess that we as patient, family, or friend sometimes feel ungrateful even when given second chances. "So what?" our attitudes shrug. We feel neglected by the rest of the family, our church, and friends; patronized by doctors; ignored by nurses; picked on by the world and even you, Lord, so that our attitude puckers in on itself like a lemon rind turned inside out.

Interrupt our discontent with reminders that we are being spared. True, we are free to fritter away second chances by being bitter at the injustice of getting sick at all; help us to know what we are choosing if we do.

Give those of us who tend and visit patience—up to a point— with those we love who seem so ungrateful for life, for healing, and even for us!

Forgive bitterness; I think it's catching. Help us to be immune to any we encounter, especially the heartbreaking cases of it in the souls of those we love and in ourselves. Help us find a way to penetrate ingratitude so it can be eradicated as effectively as any other disease. It's a deadly plague.

Words to Hold You: "Teach us to number our days, That we may present to Thee a heart of wisdom" (Psalm 90:12, NASB).

Enemy Number One

My body betrayed me by getting sick, Lord, and sometimes I hate it. I want doctors to cut it up, pull it apart, and pluck it clean of illness as if it is an enemy to be defeated, a traitor and a sneak.

Special body parts that once nourished and gave pleasure, carried us from here to there, housed our thoughts, bore our young, or pumped our life and breath have shockingly betrayed us and we feel cheated.

Yet we hear your words describing *all* you created, including us and our wondrous bodies, ". . . it was very good" (Genesis 1:31, RSV). Illness has *tainted* our bodies, not become them. Special body parts gained their beauty from *within* our spirits, not from the surface of our skins. Calm us, Lord.

Help us to get rid of the taint but not discard the body in the process, for when we move from self-loathing, fearing our own flesh, and viewing our bodies as enemies we will gain an ally: the body. Made in your image, it is meant to be well, good, strong, and it is striving always to be so.

So give us new ways of looking, seeing, and touching our bodies so we can enlist them as aids in our healing. Hold our hands in yours as we cradle ourselves and call upon the body's amazing energy and beauty, which you created to ward off intruding illness and to repair and restore.

We can defeat the pall of illness and discard sick and diseased spots, for they are not welcome in our bodies, Lord, your dwelling place. Bless this house.

Words to Hold You: "For everything created by God is good, and nothing is to be rejected . . ." (1 Timothy 4:4, NASB).

Shortchanged

With my luck, I couldn't have won the lottery, Lord. Oh, no, I got sick, not the jackpot.

We've lived good lives, been honest and upstanding, perhaps even devout—at the very least we've been nice people—and we still got sick. It's like coming up short at the bank where the coins we thought we brought in our piggy bank don't agree with the teller's total. We feel cheated, shortchanged.

Cancer, heart disease, stroke, chronic or progressive illnesses—you name them, Lord, and we have been stricken, shortchanged in the prime of life.

This is not what we'd banked on, not what we thought you'd give us as we saved up our good deeds, kind words, and thoughtful acts like change in that piggy bank.

Help us to sort this out, for illness is not like losing a heavenly lottery; wellness is not stored up "goodness" to prevent bad things like illness from happening. Believing this is making us sick in our souls, which need healing too. Help us to realize that how we lead our lives affects their quality, not necessarily their outcome, for most illnesses simply happen as randomly as rain. Help us to know that you are sad *with* us, and are helping us to overcome and heal.

What we *can* save for rainy days, Lord, instead of spiritual change, are daily conversations with you, daily acceptance of your grace and presence with us. Sick or well, this is an investment that always adds up.

Words to Hold You: "'Where your treasure is, there will your heart be also. . . . do not be anxious for your life . . .'" (Matthew 6:21-25, NASB).

Balancing Act

Timing is everything, Lord, in this balancing act of illness. We are racing back and forth between giving up and fighting. We are trying to absorb, understand, adjust to, and accept what is happening, accept its realities and possibilities. We know acceptance is part of healing, but *acceptance* of what—just death? misery?

Where is the split-second shift between accepting the fight and accepting the outcome? We want to help ourselves by knowing where to focus our energies and efforts rather than fight in vain.

Give us strength to find and face facts, for before we can *accept* them we need to know what they are; there is freedom and power in knowledge.

Help us to not give in prematurely to terminal thoughts, Lord, by thinking that passive endurance is how we are *accepting* our illness. For *accepting* is not throwing in the towel, rolling over and playing dead, giving up, or giving in. Rather, through your grace, *accepting* prepares us to fight, rallies our resources, and brings us peace and a clearer sense of purpose, like how to fight.

Acceptance is like going to the bank, Lord, to withdraw our savings; it tells us it is time to draw from our spiritual, mental, and physical resources. And you are our endless, bottomless, forever source.

Words to Hold You: "I have learned to be content in whatever circumstances I am. . . . I can do all things through Him who strengthens me" (Philippians 4:11b-13, NASB).

Doves of Hope

Illness has cast us adrift in a leaky boat on a tumultuous sea and we can see neither our destination nor landmarks. The night is dark, the stars hidden, the course uncharted; we are lost in sickness's misery.

We need doves, Lord, those messengers of hope you sent long ago to show your children the storm was nearly over. We need doves, for they ease our anxiety and remind us that you are nearby, a safe harbor.

But in such misery as this illness where do we find doves of hope? Hear our distress calls, our SOS messages from our frail crafts of body and soul being buffeted by noxious cures and uncertain prognoses.

Send doves.

Thank you, Lord, they're here!

We recognize your doves in medicines that heal; hands of doctors and nurses that tend; smiles of cleaning lady and volunteer; steadfast calm of chaplain, pastor; in the humor of a get-well card; visits from friends; prayers of family, friends, and strangers who learn of our need. We recognize them . . . all around us.

We feel this caring as if it were a breeze created from a thousand fluttering dove wings and are lifted, comforted, buoyed.

We can glimpse land, Lord, where we are restored to wellness and are vigorous and wiser. Once we've docked there, help us to *be* doves.

Words to Hold You: "He caused the storm to be still, So that the waves of the sea were hushed. . . . He guided them to their desired haven" (Psalm 107:29-30, NASB). ". . . he saw the Spirit of God descending as a dove . . ." (Matthew 3:16b, NASB).

The Power in "As If"

We face uncertain futures, Lord, when illness intrudes. We have fears and questions. But through your grace we also have options on how to be sick.

"How to be sick"—sounds silly, doesn't it? But we need to learn to be sick *as if we are going to recover* rather than *as if* we are going to die.

Two patients shared a room: One hated treatment, shunned doctors, and pulled down the window shades when she went home. The other grimaced but endured treatment, kidded doctors, led cheers on her behalf, planned next season's wardrobe, and redesigned her kitchen.

What effect did all this have? Who can say? But who felt better as illness ran its course? One is living; the other, who had a greater statistical chance, never made it through the first round of treatment.

Even though no one can actually measure the healing power of attitude, Lord, help us to add it to our roster of things we are doing to help ourselves, like prayer, treatments, and lifestyle changes. We'll use whatever we are given, knowing you work in mysterious, marvelous ways to heal.

Empowered by this assurance, we will live *as if we are recovering.* We feel you gently pulling us along the path of life toward treatments and therapies, consultations, experiments. We hear you chuckling at our jokes and applauding our business, vacation, and wardrobe plans for next year. You treat us, Lord, *as if* we deserve to get well; we will go and do likewise.

Words to Hold You: "In hope against hope he believed. . . . he did not waver in unbelief, but grew strong in faith . . ." (Romans 4:18-20, NASB).

When and If

The difference, Lord, between some of us after the diagnosis is as simple as choosing which word to live by: *when* or *if*.

Some say, *"When* death comes . . ."; others, however, holding fast to your promises of healing and renewal, say, *"If* death comes in the progression of this illness . . ." Either could tell the tale that only time can tell.

When and *if* are worlds apart—lives apart—for the one assumes that cures, remissions, and stalling death can't happen and that a grim, dreaded diagnosis *only* equals death.

Claiming that thought as the single option of response, Lord, no one's spirit has room for other possibilities. So the *"when"* becomes an inevitable, chiseled-in-concrete, no-way-out road map for what happens next instead of *"if,"* which is equally possible.

Guard us against making gigantic leaps across chasms of trouble that don't need to be leapt yet. Urge us to reconsider making only negative conclusions. Remind us to consider all options of response, such as hoping and believing that remissions happen, cures take place, death is stalled, and wellness is restored when it seems impossible at first glance.

A single word is such a simple difference, Lord, yet it can bring us volumes of comfort, energy, and determination to detour around the roadblock of thinking only *"when."* There's so much we can do with *"if."*

Words to Hold You: "For as he thinketh in his heart, so is he" (Proverbs 23:7a, KJV).

Takes One to Know One

How many springs make a lifetime, Lord? How many times of making love, baking apple cakes, swinging high in the oak tree, singing a hymn, and licking ice cream cones are *enough*?

The lump in her breast started this tallying, which came up far short of *enough*. Greedy for life, she endured tests, surgeries, exercises, and a make-do bosom. Grateful for life, she spoke to others and demonstrated the exercises and the make-do bosom to Reach for Recovery.

Bless her openness as she shows her scar to any who fear mutilation. *"Balderdash,"* she snorts, displaying a sewed up seam of healing that has given, not taken away. Bless her nagging for self-exams: "Take life into your own hands; make your husband, boyfriend, sons too."

Bless her with many more feisty days, Lord, so she can spread her message that while no number of springs is *enough*, each one is sufficient for thanksgiving for it. It is a brilliant plan, for there is no one better to remind us of this than one who knows, one who bears the scars.

Those who share from their pain are special angel messengers from you. Give us the good, grateful sense to listen, watch, and learn how to be victors. Someday perhaps we, too, can pass on this knowledge.

Bless the scarred who visit others in recovery and show us how to draw road maps from our crisscrossing scars into new routes for living, the place where you want us all to dwell.

And please, Lord, guard them against further peril.

Words to Hold You: "Every one helps his neighbor, and says . . ., 'Take courage!'" (Isaiah 41:6, RSV).

Seeds of Hope

No matter the diagnosis, prognosis, and odds, Lord, a seed of hope stirs. No matter how dark the illness, we strain toward light. No matter the obstacles that, like weeds, we must overcome, we yearn to grow into fuller flower.

From our yearning, we feel your re-creating breath blowing across our sick bodies and troubled spirits like thawing spring breezes across winter-weary gardens, and seed hope stirs stronger.

With your hand tending it, Lord, seed hope cannot be dislodged like plants before the hoes of erroneous beliefs—beliefs that we don't deserve to get well or that we are being punished by this illness or that we are victims of a willful God who would choose to make us so sick.

Nothing could be farther from the truth, for why would you intentionally give us illness with one hand and give us seeds of hope with the other? Instead, we recognize your hand beckoning us into new seasons where we may abundantly bloom and grow, not wither at your whim.

Even knowing this, it would be easy sometimes to give in to droughts of despair and hailstones of fear. And then we look around us, from potted plants and vases of flowers sent to our bedsides to trees, plants, even weeds in the parking lot, and we know that hope and a full growing season are your will.

As we recuperate a step at a time, Lord, we will be tending the seeds upon which we can grow.

Words to Hold You: "'I came that they may have life, and have it abundantly'" (John 10:10b, RSV).

Have You Heard the One About . . .?
(dedicated to Don Sexton)

"You were resting so soundly, I didn't want to disturb you, so I just tiptoed out," the visitor apologized to the patient on the next visit.

"All I needed was a lily in my hand," the patient replied, leading the laughter, for the thought was there between them. Now they had a bridge on which to more easily share concerns, share a prayer that it would not happen.

Joking, Lord, sometimes makes crying easier. It also heals.

But how can we laugh while crying? How can we tell jokes while bodies are hurting, sickness is threatening? How can we *dare* tell jokes while some hearts are slowing, eyes closing, days ending?

How can we *not* tell jokes? is the better question, for laughter heals from the inside out. It brings up chuckles and belly laughs in bodies and souls that have forgotten what it feels like to have balance in life even in the midst of illness—even, Lord, in the midst of dying.

As we face worrisome sick days, restore at least our funny bones, so we can lighten them up. Humor can help heal too, sparking hope and igniting energy with which to combat illness, ease grief.

We're not being falsely brave and putting on a "smiley face" to cover up sorrow and fear. It's just that we've cried all the tears we need to for now. We've asked all the questions and are wondering, "What now?"

"Have a good laugh." The punch line is that we all feel better after a good chuckle. Heard any good jokes lately, Lord? There's just something healing about a full-body laugh, a remarkable gift from your wisdom.

Words to Hold You: "A cheerful heart is good medicine, but a crushed spirit dries up the bones" (Proverbs 17:22, NIV).

Miraculous

We are praying for a miracle, Lord, that this illness not kill. We are praying for a miracle, but confess we don't expect it. We don't aim high enough when we pray, for we suffer from the "Lottery Syndrome": certain good things happen only to others. Why? Because we are equally certain we don't have enough faith to be worthy of the miracle we need.

Turn us around, Lord, and show us your outstretched hands overflowing with all the good things we'd ever need, *especially* the gift of faith.

Show us the miracles of remission, cures, reprieves, adaptation. Show us miracles of restored hope, of peace and strength amid chaos. Show us miracles of love, of steadfast family and friends, of indescribable caring. Show us the miracles that weren't quite what we expected but turned out miraculous anyhow in their power to transform and redeem.

Show us that miracles are on a continuum from in utero surgeries to heart transplants to "routine" miracles between. A short time ago, Lord, these were miracles as impossible as the ones we're praying for now.

Keep us aiming higher, higher when we pray, knowing that faith is not a *quantity* that can be measured—like sugar in a cup—to be either "enough" or "not enough" to get us that miracle. Rather, faith is a *gift, a quality* that says, "I believe God is for me, not against me."

The greatest miracle is *knowing* you are always *for* and *with* us.

Words to Hold You: "If God is for us, who is against us?" (Romans 8:31, RSV). "Faith is the assurance of things hoped for, the conviction of things not seen" (Hebrews 11:1, RSV).

Angels Watchin' over Me
(In memory of Caroline Keith)

"All night, all day, angels watchin' over me, my Lord. All night, all day, angels watchin' over me."

At the least-expected moment, Lord, one of your angels appears in the margins of our lives. Many have tales to share, angels to offer. Help us to listen and trust. Thank you for sending them to us, to me.

Yes, I thank you for the angelic visitor who shared Mother's bedside with me. I've never felt such warmth and peace as when I realized the angel was her traveling companion through this dark valley of illness.

Was it a dream? a wish? No, Lord. We welcome angels who come to comfort, intervene, and accompany. We pore over verses and search the heavens and corners of our sickrooms for them. We yearn for them even if we're uncertain how they'll appear. We pin jewelry replicas of them on our shirts, write notes on angel cards, and sing carols about them. We dress up like them at holidays and remind one another to "Be an angel."

Lord, can't you see from our searching how lonely we are for you to come nearer? When we do meet your angels, we are touched forever by your generous Spirit in doing just that, and we feel your love.

We welcome angels whether we can speak of them or not, for they assure us that you personally care for each of us. Send them to us in these dark moments of illness when we need more than ever a fluttering of angel love to remind us you are indeed watchin' over us.

Words to Hold You: "He will give his angels charge of you to guard you in all your ways. On their hands they will bear you up, lest you dash your foot against a stone" (Psalm 91:11-12, RSV).

Drawing Lessons

We've heard it a thousand times, Lord—that old saying, "God helps those who help themselves." Sometimes it's said to prod and accuse; other times, it's told as truth about your desire to be our companion and partner to help us along the way.

How can you help us help ourselves now that we are so ill?

We hear your questions for us: "Do you want to be healed? Do you believe you deserve to be healed?" We flinch from your hard questions, for too many of us secretly think we instead deserve illness, as if it were cosmic punishment. And it's that secret belief, dear Creator, that pokes holes in our words about wanting to be well, for our hearts aren't in it. The odds, we remind you, are against us getting well, at maybe only 40 percent.

Take our hand in yours while we draw ten stick figures as children might draw; let's pick bright colors for four of them. Guide us to write our names above one of the colorful figures, Lord, for it can be us: one of the fortunate 40 percent who get well. It has to be someone; why not us?

We hear you ask us again, finding the answer deep in our souls where we *know* you want healing and wellness for us all: "Do you believe you deserve to get well?" Hear our resounding "Yes!" as we bend to lovingly touch the bright stick figure that is us, a most deserving child who has so many God-given resources to draw upon to help it happen, for we say with the psalmist, "We are wonderfully made."

Words to Hold You: "'Truly I say to you, whoever . . . does not doubt in his heart, but believes that what he says is going to happen, it shall be granted him'" (Mark 11:23, NASB). ". . . I am fearfully and wonderfully made; . . ." (Psalm 139:14, NASB).

R & R: Recovery and Recuperation

The major crisis is past, Lord. Our fears of treatment and trauma are becoming memory, but now recovery is taking its toll! We never thought it would be this hard and scary to get well again.

Eating a little more and walking a bit farther each day wears us out and makes us worry if we are "overdoing." Everyone is pushing, pushing and we want to be left alone. Our moods are like hospital beds, crazily up one minute, flat down the next; we cry and laugh and sleep like babies.

Recovery is hard work.

It's scary too, and we walk on eggshells as we get better, fearing that the slightest jolt, sudden movement, or change in this precarious new routine will cause a relapse.

We're afraid to hold and be held too tightly for fear of "breaking." We're afraid to live with passion again for fear our hearts will stop in the middle of a loving beat. We're afraid to move, walk, laugh, lift, sit, stand, or push ourselves. But most of all, Lord, we're afraid to relax for fear illness will sneak up behind us again.

Be with us in these shaky days of getting well. Hold our hands as we navigate our way back to health. Nudge us forward through difficult therapies and exercises. And when fears come, remind us, Lord, that we are Veterans of Recovery with resources to combat any illness that dares strike again—and we have the scars to prove it! Lead us with laughter into full recovery, but carefully, for we are still a bit wobbly.

Words to Hold You: ". . . your recovery will speedily spring forth" (Isaiah 58:8a, NASB).

Walking in the Footprints

Like items named on Saturday's grocery list, Lord, there are maladies, diseases, and syndromes that plague us. Cures sometimes alter not only our bodies and minds, but also the daily routine from devices and contraptions we love/hate.

Companions make them bearable; support makes them understandable and part of our new daily routine.

"Been there; done that," they say, showing us how, and we are grateful for the examples they set even as we are terrified of the need for them. We are grateful, though, that we can find *continual* healing from the devices and contraptions that define our new selves and by following in the footprints of those who traveled this way first.

If we worry about something, they've got a solution. If we wonder, they've got an answer. Give us the *get up and go* to attend meetings, to ask questions, to learn and grow, for there was a time not long ago when we were ready to bargain with you for any chance at life. Now we have it, Lord, and we want to make the absolute most of it; help us to learn how.

We recognize you in the welcoming support and openhanded suggestions of others willing to show how we, too, can learn to live in the new ways this illness dictates. We see your hand in the clever, creative, and determined adaptations they pass on to us.

So now, Lord, give us the courage to ask for their support; there is no need to do this alone since you are with us and so are they.

Words to Hold You: "This is how we know what love is . . ." (1 John 3:16a, GNB).

Tomorrow, Tomorrow

Like the song says, Lord, thoughts of "Tomorrow, Tomorrow" fill our minds as we wonder what waits on the other side of this illness even as we are getting better.

We admit we look far beyond just one tomorrow; we anticipate *all* of them! Yet there is no way we can absorb, accept, and adapt to this fast-forwarded version of the future, and we are overloaded.

Teach us to live in today, needing just a small glimpse down the road. Help us to learn not to borrow trouble. The alternative is driving us crazy as we try to project next month, next year, the next five years.

In our anxiety we are piling up "What ifs" like boulders on the road to recovery. We can't see around them to your promise to be with us even to the end of the age—and just think how many tomorrows that will be. Forgive our frail trust when we instead demand that you show us how all the tomorrows will turn out.

If we're learning anything from being sick, Lord, it is that fear can be tamed; dread, tempered; and trust, counted on. You are a companion God.

And now as we rest quietly, we know for certain that you offer strength enough for us even the day *after* tomorrow. It will take care of itself, Lord, and we leave it and all our tomorrows in your hands.

Words to Hold You: "We live by faith, not by sight" (2 Corinthians 5:7, NIV).

Trading Stamps

I had been afraid to ask, "Why?" Lord, until I remembered the old Green Stamps we collected in a kitchen drawer and then turned in for appliances, toys, or TV trays at the redemption store.

So now I am free to ask, "Why?" "Why this illness? Why now? Why me?" But now instead of being a lament, my question is a request for direction after I am recovered and out and about again.

"Why me?" now seems the perfect question, for what I'm really asking is, "Who can I become? What can I do for others because of my experience with this illness, suffering?" What can I "trade in" these stamps of awfulness for that will redeem them into something useful?

Let illness remind us not to overlook the promised redemption hidden beneath the surface of *every* heartbreak, even beyond the sickroom. Sadly, though, as if filling drawers full of trading stamps, we seem to be collecting a lot of heartbreaks right now.

So we offer them to you, Lord. Redeem them into healed, wiser bodies; changed, healthier living; compassion and advocacy for other sufferers; renewed commitments; renegotiated relationships—whatever we need.

We are free to ask our "Why?" questions, for we know you aren't making illness happen just so we can be better persons afterward, Lord. We are grateful that you instead offer us the power to redeem it.

Words to Hold You: ". . . lay aside the old self, . . . and put on the new self, . . ." (Ephesians 4:22-24, NASB).

A Thank-You Note

Some people are healers in your style, Lord, and we are grateful even as we rage about health care in general and our illness in particular. We are feeling frightened, nitpicky, an vulnerable in the face of all these strangers poking and prodding, hurting us and our loved ones.

How angry doctors and nurses could be, Lord, at the whining, resistant patients squirming beneath their stethoscopes. How frustrated at the worried families demanding miracles, answers, and bargains.

Gentle healers are surely a gift from you sent to travel lonely roads of illness as a companion with us as patient, family. Sustain them as they sustain us in spite of ourselves; they are a channel of your love.

Be with them, for their gentleness is surely too fragile to endure all the births, deaths, and sustaining life between. We demand much from them.

Help them to know we aren't intentionally ungrateful when we forget to say, "Thanks." We are just distracted. Help them to understand that the homemade jellies or store-bought candies and the family pictures we send in Christmas cards are the only ways we can think of to thank them.

Help them to continue to be gentle with us in our worst moments, for their tending to us provides a healer's touch of unmeasurable power that is far beyond mere pill and potion.

And, Lord of countless unsung acts of healing, remind us to send those cards, make those jellies. It is healing for us to be thankful.

Words to Hold You: ". . . let us love one another; for love is of God, . . ." (1 John 4:7, RSV).

When illness brings good-bye . . .

Left Behind

I can't find the Christmas card list, Lord . . . or the new box of checks.

While hunting, though, I found piles of *stuff* beneath beds, on closet shelves, and in the garage, basement, and car trunk. But there are no clues as to what this dearly beloved person intended to do with it. There are no clues, either, to the meaning behind messages on the calendar.

So much of our lives is shorthand, Lord, and we rely on others to solve daily puzzles, but they are gone, leaving us and mysteries behind.

Why were we left behind like an outgrown jacket crumpled on the closet floor? unfinished messages on a calendar? *stuff* in the garage?

Anger has returned and sits atop this unfinished and unfinishable *stuff*. We thought we'd chased anger away in that first raging at illness's intrusion. Help us to accept it again; it's OK to feel wildly mad, for quiet, sodden bereavement is too passive for the enormity of our loss.

Help us learn to at least chuckle at the mysteries left in this jumble as if it were a scavenger hunt of our life. Help us to not need answers as much as memories of the delightful person who *made* the mystery and left the *stuff*!

Help us to understand *we* are not leftovers like unfinished socks on knitting needles or cars disassembled in the garage. We were mourned as we were left with this *stuff*. Lord, reassure us that the new anger spilling over as we sort, pack, and cart away is a transient visitor. It is here only as a temporary bridge to somewhere else, not to trip over forever.

Words to Hold You: "He gives strength to the weary and increases the power of the weak" (Isaiah 40:29, NIV).

Photo of Love

In a coat pocket is a photograph brought from home to the hospital today. See the smiling face in the photo? *This* is my special mate, not the frail and ill person propped in a bed. What a wonderful day we had when that photograph was taken—a picnic day filled with laughter, play, promise.

It is *this* person, Lord, the one preserved in a colored square, being mourned in farewell, not the shadow one in the bed who is ready to come home to be with you where all days are picnic-bright days. It is time, Lord, time.

Welcome both, Lord—the laughing, picnicking partner and the patient being sent home on wings of memory and prayers of thankfulness for a shared life, for picnics, even for rainy days together.

Knowing you've been there with both, just as at this leave-taking and the joyous someday reunion picnic, makes it bearable to be left only with a smiling photograph of a person loved so dearly, sending the spirit on ahead.

Words to Hold You: (Psalm 34:18, RSV)."The LORD is near to the brokenhearted, and saves the crushed in spirit"

Take Enough Time

Should I sell the house or reroof and stay? Should I even stay in the neighborhood or simply move away? Should I liquidate or invest?

Not only is it not easy to make decisions after a mate's death, Lord, it is dangerous, for we aren't certain what we are doing. We fear we'll regret later a decision made in haste, but are tired of feeling helpless. We want to affect our futures, however lonely they may be.

Perhaps, we chuckle, we should make no decisions more binding than what kind of salad dressing to have for supper or what flavor ice cream for dessert! We careen like untied balloons let loose to fly across the room, hitting one wall, then another as memory, moods, and dread send us hither and yon in frantic, erratic loop-de-loops.

While we are so fragile and unpredictable, give us the good sense to stall, Lord, in those matters that can wait. Teach us to put off until tomorrow that which we shouldn't dare attempt today. Reassure us this is only temporary, a brief hesitation, not a giving up. Hold up a mirror for us to see once again a clear-eyed person who can—and does—decide.

For now, Lord, stay with us as we choose "plain vanilla" and "basic oil and vinegar." This is as complicated as it gets today, and that is OK. There will be tomorrows, and we'll be ready, having spent today healing.

Words to Hold You: "He will swallow up death for ever, and the LORD God will wipe away tears from all faces . . ." (Isaiah 25:8, RSV).

A Gathering Circle

Like old home movies rewound and shown over again, tales are told by the family gathered at the bedside. An hour ago, Lord, we'd had hope for recovery. Now that's outdated news, a final coma having said amen to it.

We're here now instead to offer our best last gesture: the gift of a fond farewell. Be with us as we do, Lord, because telling the tale when the end is already in sight hurts so much.

"Remember when?" we say, Lord, laughing, interrupting one another in the retelling of times shared with this special one who may yet hear us, smiling in deep sleep at our once-upon-a-time tales.

"Remember when?" We savor a final showing, reel upon reel, of pranks pulled, triumphs achieved, kindnesses shown, conversations held. "Remember when?"

And now, bringing a last frame into focus, "Remember when we talked of life forever after? of rooms prepared for us? You'll be the first of us there, and while we shrink against daily life without you, we're comforted knowing you've just gone on ahead. Go," we whisper. "We'll be along shortly to finish the rest of this remembering tale. As long as we have memory, it is not ended, merely continued."

Thank you, Lord, for the gift of memory to our days ahead, of being able to "remember when," a powerful resource to daily fill this absence.

Words to Hold You: "You will be blessed when you come in and blessed when you go out" (Deuteronomy 28:6, NIV).

Funerals: The Best of Intentions

We dread this ordeal of the funeral, memorial service, and don't know if we can endure it. Is it necessary? healing? good to do?

Others insist, Lord, so be with us in receiving lines, on hard pews and chairs; be with us as we stand frozen with souls of winter amid the summer bouquets of wreaths, sprays, and planters; be with us at graves where we are leaving part of ourselves behind—dust to dust, ashes to ashes.

We want to do more than endure, Lord, and pray these moments will help heal our terrible grief. Transform the brief gathering of loved ones into a ritual about living, not about dying.

Help us to find creative ways to grieve within this community of caring. Perhaps we can open photo albums or surround ourselves with the favorite music, books, or paintings of the one who is gone; maybe we can set out samples of hobbies and an old fishing hat, a quilt, or a plant tended. Remembrances, Lord, to comfort us all.

Help us to understand that this event is not the last stop on our journey of loss, but rather the first step on our journey of recovery. This gathering with its names in a register and blurred faces in lines is one more resource, like photo albums and boxes of collectibles, that will help us find our path beyond death and out of the cemetery. Its intention is just that.

Words to Hold You: "Therefore comfort one another . . ."
(1 Thessalonians 4:13-18, RSV).

Too Loud a Silence: A Child Dies
(in memory of Kelly and David)

No birthday songs to sing, Lord, no presents to wrap, no cards to sign . . . the birthday child, forever young, will attend today's family gathering in spirit only, for illness snatched the body from our grasp.

O Lord, can there be a greater parental grief? Death of a child, no matter the age, is incomprehensible and impossible to prepare for. It is an obscenity against nature, and we wail in protest.

But what else are we, the friends and family, to do now? We don't know, so after a time we do little. Forgive us that you are often the only one who hears the dead child's name spoken. Forgive us when you are the only one who witnesses the rending of parents' hearts as they turn away from each other, from family and friends, other children, from us.

Thank you, God of compassion, for groups where parents' grieving can be what it is: an action verb. Bless fellow sufferers who listen when the rest of the world, embarrassed and uneasy, turns away from tears.

Inspire and equip the rest of us not to forget a relative or friend's lost child, but instead speak the beloved name aloud; remind us to send a card on birth and death anniversaries. Remind us not to turn away at tears or the mention of a dead child's name. Make us stronger than that, for ours is the easiest burden; we only have to be embarrassed.

And, Lord, remind us not to let illness have the last word, but to donate, volunteer, advocate in this child's name. Send us to reassure bereaved parents that their children may be gone, but not forgotten.

Words to Hold You: "If they are sad, share their sorrow" (Romans 12:15b, TLB).

Briefly Ever After

Unknown, but not unloved, is this tiny child cradled in the double circle of a mother's and father's arms. A double circle of love surrounds this beloved child planned, practiced for, and prayed over from conception. A circle of love, though, not strong enough to hold onto life against illness's pull, and this little one died as it was born.

Was this little one ever out of your sight while sliding into waiting parents' arms? Was he, she, ever beyond your care? Were you weeping, too, with the parents at the stillness sounding such a wrong note in the delivery room?

Comfort all who were touched by this little life nestled so lovingly in a soft blanket and going-home clothes so carefully pressed and ready. The parents, Lord—give them the memories they've earned . . . of joyful conception, of first "butterfly" quickening, of diaper practicing, of painting a sunlight yellow nursery. Let no one tamper with that joy now overtaken by sorrow; both tell the tale of this child so briefly theirs. Comfort the rest of the family waiting outside the closed door; give them forthright grief that includes naming this child as grandchild, brother, sister. Let no one diminish this precious life by denying her, him, a memory.

This little one is unknown, Lord, but not unloved.

Words to Hold You:"'I have called you by name, you are mine'" (Isaiah 43:1b, RSV).

A Poem for the Journey

It's not really very good poetry, Lord, but it's penned with midnight oil by a grieving parent who cannot sleep. The subject is always the same, and all words eventually rhyme with *child, miss you,* and *lonely.*

Struck down by illness in the prime of life—long past the days when parents worry about kids crossing streets, getting sick, dying too early—this child's death has left a grown-up sized void that can only be filled up with rhyming words. Let them speak for all who suffer this loss.

Comfort the mothers and fathers who had relaxed their parental vigilance over offspring now grown to adulthood, for they now reel from assumptions of safety suddenly revoked.

Comfort them, too, from those who come to console and offer solace only to take it away with careless remarks: "Oh, but losing an adult child is not as bad as losing a young child."

Not true, Lord, not true, and these bereft parents recoil from any sentiment that suggests love has a calendar that can ever be filled with enough days spent with a child of any age.

It's such a shock to lose an adult child. You know how it is, and we weep now in the full awareness of your understanding.

From your great wellspring of compassion, comfort these parents with the rich resource of memory, of seeing the fruits of their labors at least partially fulfilled. And as you bring to them your oft-promised comfort, lighten their particular hard, dark grief.

Words to Hold You: "Your sun shall no more go down . . . and your days of mourning shall be ended" (Isaiah 60:20, RSV).

Children's Moment

What can we tell the children, Lord, when death interrupts the innocence of childhood? Their upturned faces, so like flowers, are waiting eagerly for us to tell them why the one they loved isn't here, why we're sad.

Inspire us as you did your Son to gather little ones to our knee. Remind us to respect them as he did and you do us; remind us not to talk down to them, nor lie, nor scare them lest they assume they and their questions are causing our distress.

"Why?" they ask. We can share our need to know why too, plus our acceptance that sometimes there are no easy answers. We can ask *them* a "why" question: why are we together talking about this special person? To remember and celebrate, for two heads are better than one at doing both, something children already know about the joy of community.

Guide our words so we can help them discover that "together" is the best place for tough times, that shared grief and mutual questions offer comfort and sanctuary from life-and-death riddles. Where two or three are gathered, Lord, here you are, even in the midst of the unanswerable.

The best answer we can offer, dear children, is that this special one lived, died, and now lives on as spirit with us here in ways we name now . . .

Be with us, Lord, as we mourn our loss and celebrate the life we held so dear. Hear our childlike prayers.

Words to Hold You: ". . . comfort yourselves together . . ." (1 Thessalonians 5:11, KJV).

Childhood's End

It is not natural, Lord, that children die.

Nature invests all its energy into bringing young to full growth, from tiniest seed to mightiest whale, and our children, grandchildren between. A child's death is against all nature. Why is it happening?

This child is dying, and we have no words to speak of this to you. Our hearts are as barren as fire-swept forests, and we have no tears left to cry that could bring anything green growing there again. We ask only for your presence with this little one and us; give us courage to let go.

Help us to remember times we didn't put off playing, listening, or sharing a discovery, thought, question. Help us make peace with those times we did put off, for we travel by the light we have at the time, Lord, and who could have known how quickly and rudely this moment of loss would arrive?

We are grateful we kept time with this child as if each moment was leading to many more. How sad had we doled out time in miserly ways, for zest is the *natural* way to live with children, and we did, thank God. It made our time together seamless and fine like a quilt to lay across our bed.

Comfort us with memories like images stitched on this quilt. It's not enough, but better than the nothing we'd thought to be left holding.

Cover us with this warm quilt so when we awake, although alone, we'll not be quite so chilled. For from its remembered warmth where this child snuggled, dreams will bring our young one to us in days, years to come. It's not as good as the real thing, Lord, but enough to get us through, day by day.

Words to Hold You: "The LORD *is near to the broken-hearted . . ." (Psalm 34:18, RSV).*

Dueling with Ourselves

On one hand, Lord, we want healing for our loved one and will do anything to bring about a full recovery. *Hear our prayer of petition.*

On the other hand, Lord, we want the ordeal over and done with. No more prolonging the agony—anyone's agony. *Hear our prayer of confession.*

We're startled by the many sides to our thoughts and prayers as death draws near yet not near enough for anyone's comfort. Are we terrible for wanting resolution? Are we going to regret it after we've forgotten these suffering days? We worry about our limited loving.

Yet who in his or her right mind and soul would *want* to prolong a loved one's agony? Who would *want* to suffer alongside of that dear one if there were any other way? We know you are a God of mercy who welcomes an end to suffering too. Stay close by while we all wait it out.

Protect us from needless guilt afterward, for we don't want loved ones dead; we want them healed and at peace. And if death is to be that final healing, that place of peace, then all we ask is that you let it come quickly.

For ourselves, Lord, thank you for reassuring us that we are not weak, terrible, or wrong for wanting relief. Most of all, we want to know our loved ones are finally all right and no longer suffering what we cannot fix.

Words to Hold You: "This God is our God for ever and ever; he will be our guide even to the end" (Psalm 48:14, NIV).

Face to the Wall: Time to Go
(Dedicated to Robert Keith, Sr.)

There comes a time when the ones we love have tried as hard as they're going to. They've eaten the last spoon of pudding, turned a cheek the last time for shots, alcohol rubs, diapering, prodding. They've gritted teeth one last time against pain, aches, and pep talks.

No thanks, Lord, no more medical meddling; it's time to be done. *"Close up your little black bags and go home, docs,"* they've tried to joke. *"No,"* they insist when anyone dares push a feeding tube so much as inside the door.

Accept them when they know it's time to turn over in stiff beds with tight-tucked corners and rest, face to the wall. *"Enough,"* Lord, can you hear them say. *"Enough."*

Be with us as we tearfully, lovingly accept and support, for death is not their enemy to prevail against now. Rather the enemy is charts with procedures for tomorrow—or politeness that prevents them from throwing us cheerleaders out of the room! The enemy is weakness, and they must save enough strength to turn over, face to the wall.

For they see you beyond the wall, knowing it instead as a doorway into your waiting, cradling care whether anyone believes it or not. Take their hands; they've been waiting long enough.

And as you do, Lord, comfort us who watch and weep from doorways and beside beds. Despite our resistance, help us to respect their timing; share with us their vision of a beckoning comfort just beyond the wall.

Words to Hold You: "For everything there is a season and a time . . .: a time to be born, and a time to die"
(Ecclesiastes 3:1-2a, RSV).

Rejects

After the diagnosis "terminal," many have stopped coming into this sickroom. Vaguely embarrassed, they make us feel as if we, the patient and family, are responsible for figuring out how to handle *their* grief. Lord, we can't do it for anyone else.

Our loved ones may be dying, but is that the last word of friendship, of family time? of medical tending? Much more can yet be said.

We are grieved anew by people who act as if it's all over—no need to do anything except avoid any uncomfortable feelings that crop up. But we need companions both for letting go and planning the future.

What an opportunity missed, Lord, because healing to the reality of dying is as important a step as there can be, not only for our special loved ones, but for the rest of us too. No distance is far enough, no last line on a chart final enough to bypass a dying, for it is an active verb.

Strengthen friends, family, and caregivers, for they are desperately needed even though battles are being lost that we wanted to win. Call them back to this room for the last healing; guide their hands to hold ours in a shared circle of care.

Bind up all our hearts with the comfort found in one another's presence, Lord; it's not good for anyone to be alone in moments like these.

Words to Hold You: "You have been my help; don't leave me, don't abandon me. . . . Have faith, do not despair" (Psalm 27:9b-14, GNB).

Riddle Me a Riddle

This illness, Lord, has run its course; *terminal* is the label added to it now and death looms on the horizon. What happens when we die? We are so afraid not knowing; send us comforting hints, assurances.

Lord, are you answering us through a child? When her friend died, the three-year-old immediately asked, "Did he change houses?"

"Changing houses" may be as good an explanation of death as any, for we don't know exactly what happens when we arrive on your doorstep, but getting a new house feels OK.

"Does God tuck us in? read us stories? Does God have a lap we can sit on? Does God sing us lullabies when we're scared?" the child persisted.

We're grateful for the child's questions, for they mirror our own, even if spoken in unsophisticated words. We all want to be found, be home, be safe.

Help us to believe and accept comfort in simple, childlike possibilities, for little ones who sit close to your knee may understand best:

They *know* you would not leave your children, like a dolly or teddy bear, out in the rain or homeless once we've left our other houses. They *know* you have eternal treats and forever joy in store for us. They know your lap is an "always" kind of comfort where lullabies begin even now. If we lie still in childlike trust we can hear faint music.

Guide our journey home, Lord, to the new house you have prepared.

Words to Hold You: "In my Father's house are many rooms; . . . I go to prepare a place for you . . ., that where I am you may be also" (John 14:2-3, RSV).

Homecoming Too Soon
(in memory of Bobby Keith)

Time helps, Lord, but it never quite blunts the loneliness.

Time ran out for the tormented souls of our loved ones. Consumed by despair, they forfeited their claim on life and chose death at their own hand. We cry anew at our loss and the force of their misery.

Can there be a greater shock than in the abandonment felt by those of us left behind? a greater guilt? more confusing anger?

Help us to forgive ourselves for real or imagined mistakes. Help us to know it wasn't us they wanted to leave, but rather their own torment that also made them forget who they were leaving: us.

Thank you for forgiving them, Lord; we are learning to. Thank you for the compassion we see cradling them in a peace they never had here.

It is lonely being left like this. The burden to carry on alone bends us over as did that first grief and we feel starkly alone and often marooned. We feel you move closer; thank you.

Thank you for the gift of dreams of them as they once were: hopeful, whole, and with us. We cherish these dreams and memories, for they keep our grief balanced. Thank you, too, for dreams of them now: restored and healed of the crushing depression that simply squashed life.

We rely on your grace, Lord, and strong homecoming hands that caught them as they fell that great distance down the pit of despair. Thank you for reaching out for them as they fell, sons and daughters of yours who came home too soon.

Words to Hold You: *"'DEATH IS SWALLOWED UP in victory. . . . O DEATH, WHERE IS YOUR STING?'"* *(1 Corinthians 15:51-55, NASB).*

Parting Shots

There are those in our lives we will not mourn when they are gone, for they have hurt us. On one hand, Lord, are the little hurts of rudeness, misunderstandings. Give us the good sense to forgive them as you do us.

On the other hand, an enemy is dying and we are relieved. Help us.

How can we say good-bye to sources of big hurts—the abusers, batterers, crooks, rapists, killers, drunks? How can we say a proper good-bye to an enemy, a traitor, especially—as most are—someone we call family?

What are we to do with the evidence of their wrongdoing? Is it possible to bury terrible deeds with the doers so that we not continue their legacy of violence as perpetual victims? Show us ways to do it, Lord.

Be with us as we approach their bedsides in our minds, seeing them for what they are: victims of their own misused lives. Help us hand back to them what they've done to us so we do not pass it on in our lives.

We hand you the gavel of judgment we've carried around. Accountability, charges, and punishment are one thing, Lord; vengeance is another, and we want to be freed of our hunger for it.

Be with us as we forgive them. Stay close by, for they must be lonely; be ready should they be sorry.

And now be with us as we say good-bye, mourning what could have been if others' choices had been different. Go with us as we leave the bedside of a former enemy, freed, healed, forgiven, and forgiving . . . no longer victims, just veterans with no more need to prolong the battle.

Words to Hold You: "Create in me a clean heart, O God, And renew a steadfast spirit within me" (Psalm 51:10, NASB).

DNR: Giving and Taking Away

What a marvel are modern machines, Lord. They allow us to romp on the moon, traverse the world in hours, and keep people breathing long beyond when they can do it themselves or even want to.

Our family-medical conferences yield the code "DNR" on our loved ones' charts, promising that living or dying will be unimpeded by good intentions and heroic measures. What a decision to have to make, Lord.

As we face these moments, forgive the hesitant who fear playing God; forgive the hasty who do likewise. Forgive transgressions on both sides of the issue, giving up and holding on at wrong times.

In this high-tech age, give us some guidelines for how God would "play God." Nudge us to some sense of rightness so that we do not let our loved ones needlessly, painfully linger while we are between choices.

Guide physicians who guide us through the complex valley of medical shadows. Guide our loved ones to give us a signal long before the hour of decision; guide communication within families.

Bless the foresighted who early share their desires, Lord. Bolster our courage so we, when our time begins hastening on, can write firmly in our own hand "DNR" or otherwise, relieving loved ones from having to decide for us.

We are grateful that no matter which we do, you are a God of mercy and everlasting compassion; comfort us as we decide what your will is. No one is equipped to "play God" but you, and often how you would is muffled and faint. Show us; speak clearly, for we want only to do your bidding.

Words to Hold You: "God is . . . always ready to help in times of trouble. So we will not be afraid . . ." (Psalm 46:1-2, GNB).

Fathers' Days
(in memory of Robert and Bud)

As I stand beside this final resting place, dozens of memories flash through my mind, each a "Father's Day." And today is the last one, Lord, for my father died, leaving me alone and now the older generation.

We feel cheated when this comes too soon but confess it is always too soon; we are never ready for the changing of generations. We are never ready to let our fathers go, no matter how ready they may be.

Guide us through memory now, Lord, to our first knowledge of this man we called Father, Dad, Pop, Daddy, or some special nickname of our own creation. We recall bridges we built so we wouldn't lose touch. It's easy for kids to "misplace" a father when we're young and foolish. Thank you for all the "Father and Children Days" we shared. We will miss them.

Guide us now into a future where we will call upon his fatherly wisdom in memory only, muttering under our breath, "Dad, what do you think?" Reassure us that to mourn and remember will only make him the more dear, that to grieve and go on is what he would wish.

Comfort us, Lord, when we clean out his garage and basement to sort out his life, for fishing poles aren't supposed to have dust and cobwebs on them and fathers aren't supposed to be gone. Tears keep getting in our way as we work.

Hold me as I yearn to keep him present in my heart. Show me how.

Words to Hold You: "He has sent me to . . . comfort all who mourn . . ." (Isaiah 61:1b-2, NASB).

Sometimes I Feel like a Motherless Child

I need to ask my mother the color of my first bicycle, Lord. I need to ask her . . . I need to ask her dozens of things, but I'm too late. My mother just died and I don't know the answers to many questions I never got around to asking, but especially who I am now, how I'm to go on?

Will you finish the punch lines I've forgotten of the jokes she loved to tell? Will you help me remember relatives' names and connections? What was the address of the first house where I lived? the year and model of the car I first drove? the color of that first bike?

Reach out to me, a child again, lost, frightened, and alone with few answers for comfort. Stay with me until I fall asleep and be here if I awake scared. Let me be a child tonight, Lord. Tomorrow I'll be big and strong and all grown-up, but for now, find me, hold me.

And, Lord, visit me on my birthdays and holidays when the phone is silent, the mailbox empty. Be my family.

Words to Hold You: "Peace I leave with you; my peace I give to you . . ." (John 14:27, RSV).

Uprooted

Life isn't going to be the same; a grandparent has died, Lord. Life is already less exciting and interesting, for grandparents know all sorts of things not only about the "good old days," but about us, our roots and connections to "way back when." We are their living legacy, Lord; they are our living family tree.

When a generation dies, Lord, the entire family tree feels as uprooted and shaky as I do now. As offshoots, we worry that modern winds of scattered, split-apart family styles will topple us now that our roots are gone.

It doesn't matter that they were older or maybe ready to be home with you; we didn't want to let them go. Bonds with grandparents are surely among the strongest you created.

We loved one another unreservedly, with awe and an understanding the middle generation has forgotten on one hand and has yet to learn on the other! We have been made forever richer from sitting at gnarled knees and storytellers' sides; there was always room for us.

Comfort us as a grandparent would, pulling us onto a loving lap.

Words to Hold You: "LORD, THROUGH ALL the generations you have been our home! . . . you are God without beginning or end" (Psalm 90:1-2, TLB).

Road Maps and Night-lights

No matter what grief experts and well-wishers say about "stages of loss" and "tomorrow being another day," there seems to be nothing but emptiness ahead, Lord. At least when we had the illness to focus on, we could put off this moment; when we had memorials and rituals to make sure we got right, we could avoid looking into the blankness ahead.

Life has gone on without our mates, our best friends, but we can't.

And even if we could, or wanted to, where would we go, Lord? We have no destination, no sense of direction. The road into the future looms endlessly like a giant maze; nowhere along its route do we see signposts.

There ought to be road maps when such a loss comes, for we're left spinning vainly like weather vanes atop shared lives that used to be.

Point us in a direction. Beckon us with tales of others who've traveled in darkness like desert nomads we read of who could *only* travel in the dark of night because of the heat. They sewed tiny brass candleholders on their shoes, lighting candles for their journeys. No matter how great a distance or dark a night, they always had enough light for the next step.

We take heart from their creativity, knowing you will inspire us, too, to find innovative ways to move on. You will provide us road maps in the lives of others, the resource of memory, the lure of possibilities.

Thank you, Lord, for light to take the next step; it's all we need right now.

Words to Hold You: ". . . God is light; in him there is no darkness at all" (1 John 1:5, NIV).

Flowers for the Grave

As we signal a turn, we drive back through cemetery entrances. Traffic waits. Our headlights split the dusk as death has split our lives, Lord.

Mourners returning long after funeral flowers have faded, we visit this community of headstones as lonely widowers and widows, come to call on companions rather than face an empty house and silent meal.

We visit as parents, friends, children, grandchildren, neighbors here to collect pieces of ourselves, for we are diminished by the leave-taking of a loved one; we shrink in the loneliness and are most happy in this place.

Yet on all sides of our precious ones, Lord, signs of well-worn devotion share other mourners' histories: a schoolteacher's upright and prim signature; a child's own first-printing name on a marble stone, with her marble dollhouse nearby; flags for soldiers and sailors who now rest from wars' alarms.

Help us to find comfort in the knowledge that other mourners came, wept, and then went on with the rest of their lives, for they are not here. Help us to do likewise. Fulfill your promises that comfort comes to us who mourn. Lead us through this shadowy valley inhabited by granite markers, fading bouquets, and our crushing grief as if we, too, are buried.

Send us back into the land of living. When it's time, go with us to buy flowers for our dining tables along with flowers for the graves we visit.

Polish our memories of loved ones laid to rest here, Lord, and then strengthen our resolve for going on without them, which in itself would be a noble monument to their memory.

Words to Hold You: ". . . winter is past, the rain is over and gone. The flowers appear on the earth . . ." (Song of Solomon 2:11-12, RSV).

Lost and Found

Find me today, Lord, for I am lost between the cracks of life and death. I'm lost between who I once was and who I will become when reunited with you, a promise like a bright light drawing me through this cave of illness shadows where I no longer can remain.

I'm ready to go but not ready to leave, and this in-between time is the hardest as I reconcile myself to these being final days.

Thank you for being with me through treatments, decisions. Thank you for being the Rock on which my family rests in exhausted hoping. Thank you that acceptance of death does not mean the absence of hope, but rather its promised harvest as you speak to me of what lies ahead.

Yet, like a trapeze artist, Lord, it's not possible to grab the beckoning bar while clinging to this present one. How hard it is to let go and move on, arching through the unknown to reach your outstretched hand.

Help me to release my hold on what lies both behind and around me still, wonderful though it is, and go on. Help those I'm leaving to understand I am excited about the journey even as I mourn the saying of good-bye; one can't happen without the other.

Give them a glimpse of you catching me in your arms as I lean toward you, for I yearn to be safe and secure on the other side of this abyss. Comfort them with the knowledge that I will be there with you, too, to welcome them to the other side when it's time.

Hold out your arms, Lord; I'm moving toward you.

Words to Hold You: "The eternal God is your dwelling place, and underneath are the everlasting arms" (Deuteronomy 33:27, RSV).

What to Do While Waiting

They call it "progressive illness," Lord, and mine has "progressed" about as far as I can bear. I dream of how your final healing will come. How wonderful for some of us to be called home while listening to a glorious sonata! How wonderful to be called home while walking on the shore, a mountain, or bustling city street we love. How wonderful to be called home in our sleep.

Yet as final illnesses gather strength from weakening bodies, going home obviously isn't so easy. Sometimes we are crazy with the thought that all we have ahead is simply getting worse, sicker, more dependent, less ourselves, more afraid, more limited.

What *is* there to look forward to, Lord, while we are losing our own race? What can we do while waiting for your call to come home?

Help us to find comfort for waiting in listening to music we love—jazz; big band; rock and roll; a little Elvis, perhaps; that sonata. Let the healing rhythms soothe our worries and gentle our ravaged bodies.

Help us to find comfort as we close our eyes and, in the mind's eye, walk beach or mountain trails we've loved or float in canoes we've paddled through crystal streams where we see your sky-blue heaven reflected on their surfaces. We each have our waiting places, Lord; guide us to them.

Hold us there, for we gratefully feel your gentle presence. We yearn for you to come closer and carry us on. While we are waiting, we will use our minds and memories to relax and calm our weary selves, poised and ready to accept your invitation to come home.

Words to Hold You: "The night is nearly over; . . ."
(Romans 13:12a, NIV).

Likely Last Time

This is likely the last time I will be watching snow drift, rain puddle, leaves clutter; the last time I will bask in summer's sunlight, for I am in my final season of this life.

For a long time I wasn't interested in any good news except total recovery. Now I welcome the good news of your presence, Lord, and accept the good news of promised release from pain. It's not the best news, but good news, for it opened my mind and heart to savor the likely last times.

Naming this reality is healing for me, not depressing, although I am still grievously sad to be leaving. Nevertheless, I am savoring the doing of all sorts of wondrous things I've been too busy to even notice before; a million, a billion, daily marvels bring a smile to my face.

Through your grace, Lord, rather than thinking how sad it is that I've missed them before, I am delighted to be seeing, doing them now. It's never too late to be a joyful explorer.

Can there be anything more beautiful than a snowflake? raindrop? scarlet leaf? the faces, voices, scents of loved ones? Can there be anything more amazing than the clever ways your children have figured out how to live, work, and play together? Miracles of love fly all around me!

And, if by a healing power, I am around to celebrate this season next year, so much the better, for I will have learned how to truly savor each snowflake, raindrop, falling leaf, smile— how to live each moment. Who would have thought, Lord, that last times could be such rich seasons of discovery?

Words to Hold You: "We live by faith, not by sight" (2 Corinthians 5:7, NIV).

Love's Legacy

My life is dwindling away before I'm finished parenting my children. I want to leave them something from me—more than fading photographs and home videos that last only hours, Lord.

Inspire me to find ways to stay a part of their lives even after I'm gone, for they need to know how much I loved being a parent to them. Give me strength to carry this off and provide me with friends and family to help put hands and feet to my last wishes of a legacy of living love.

I feel your inspiration, Lord, in the idea of leaving birthday cards for each future year to be mailed for me. I will enclose a note and perhaps a small token—something they collect or will connect with our moments together—so they will know I am forever with them in spirit.

I'll leave a wedding gift too—a wonderful idea! It will be "something borrowed, old, or new," but not "something blue," for I want them to remember me as joyful in the honor of giving, sharing their life. I want them to look forward when they think of me, not only back to mourn.

I'll collect and make a treasure box filled with their baby book, first drawings, toys of mine and theirs, tiny clothes with notes of where we went the day they wore them and the fun we had.

May the comforting pleasure I get from doing this find its way into the things I leave for those I already miss dreadfully. As they receive them, Lord, may they feel we are in reunion, knowing I loved them yesterday, today, and tomorrow.

Words to Hold You: ". . . love is as strong as death . . ."
(Song of Solomon 8:6, RSV).

Reunion

"Is that you, Mama?" they heard her ask in a suddenly happy voice, and looked around in vain, for no one else could see the friendly face she was smiling at in her sleep.

Her mama came to find her today on the wings of messengers who arranged the reunion beside her deathbed. We who wait and watch at loved ones' bedsides, Lord, are touched and comforted when we become honored guests at these reunions with messengers who come calling.

Are they caused by medications? pain? illness? wishes?

Perhaps, Lord, but they could just as well be "caused" by your love for us through a natural part of creation, for you are in constant companionship with your children in ways too marvelous to comprehend.

We who can't see the messengers but do believe are comforted by the joy and relief our loved ones find when their hands are taken by a mama, papa, a child, or a friend who has come to show that the place they are going is filled with a love so strong it can bridge even the gap of death.

We take comfort in that truth even as we grieve its necessity.

Words to Hold You: "I am sure that neither death, nor life . . ., nor anything else in all creation, will be able to separate us from the love of God . . ." (Romans 8:38-39, RSV).

Today I Hope for . . .

As illness progresses, Lord, I am discovering new hope just when I thought all hope was gone! And, amazingly, as death approaches in the final healing, hope is stronger than when illness began. Then hope was for only one thing: complete recovery, certainly a worthy hope, but not always possible given the extent of disease.

If I can't have that, is there nothing left to hope for?

Only if hoping is mere wishing, which it is not, for in your wisdom you provided that hope changes as disease changes, but is never gone.

Help me to find new goals for my final illness. With you to inspire, I can find new things to hope for never considered before, new ways to settle. As I do, this renegotiated hope will provide renewed strength to do what has to happen next.

So if full recovery isn't to be, let us hope for *many* years, months. And if not many, then *several*; if not several, then *as many as needed* to finish last acts we've begun. We can also hope for less pain, Lord, hope for a peaceful death, hope the family will be OK, hope for a visitor, hope tonight sleep is easier than last night.

I accept your promise that there is *never* a time of no hope regardless of how sick I become. In the midst of this comforting, strengthening promise, I hope, most of all, Lord, that you will continue to stay close by.

Words to Hold You: "We have this hope as an anchor for the soul, firm and secure" (Hebrews 6:19a, NIV).

Breath of Life

We watch in agony as our loved ones shower, shave, and shuffle through each valuable day, Lord, tethered to one end of an oxygen tank, the last link between life and death. Heart failure, lung disease, emphysema—the causes are many, the outcome the same: no breath.

Caught in a death grip by the primitive terror of suffocating, they have a question we, too, are both reluctant and eager to ask you between the ten-second burps of oxygen: how much longer?

Please, Lord, in these last weeks or months, open windows in their imaginations. Throw wide the shutters of dreams so they can breathe in deeply of your calming presence. Blow cool breezes across sweaty foreheads as if it is your hand smoothing the furrowed lines of anxiety and dread of the next choking attack. Let them smell rain-washed pavements of memory that return them to quieter, easier afternoons before illness grabbed them around the throat.

When it is time to relinquish this life, remind them that there will be breaths deep enough for leaping and singing in their spacious and airy new home. Visit them with a windstorm of its promise, Lord, for there is just enough breath to reach for your hand.

Words to Hold You: ". . . He Himself gives to all life and breath . . .; in Him we live and move and exist . . ., 'For we also are His offspring'" (Acts 17:25-28, NASB).

End-time Pain: A Bon Voyage Gift

In the end time, Lord, pain can be one of your greatest gifts to us even as we curse and resist it.

What else but this end-time pain could unclasp the hands of a dying person from a tenacious hold to this mortal life? What else but this pain could convince loved ones to unclasp their hold on their stricken one?

Once we feel end-time pain's searing presence, guide us to use all the pain-relieving medications and methods available, for you don't want us to suffer needlessly. We've gotten pain's message—that the body is preparing for a final effort.

Help us to think of this end-time pain as a kind of "birthing pain," Lord, for we *are* in the process of becoming new beings. Help us as we labor to deliver ourselves onto that other shore, newly born and newly healed from this life's travail. Give us a hand to squeeze, for pain's waves are building themselves into a sea strong enough for us to walk across at last.

Words to Hold You: "Come to me, all who labor and are heavy laden, and I will give you rest" (Matthew 11:28, RSV).

Even Good Quality Wears Out

Bodies wear out with time, Lord, and illness speeds it up. We worry as life becomes measured by *quantity*, not *quality*: his heart is jump-started by a battery; her meal is served through a tube; machines breathe for both.

Lord, is this living? Is this your promised abundant life?

Yes, on one hand, it is and we celebrate a *quantity* of days with our aging loved ones and the medical marvels that extend it. On the other, *quality of life* asks for a chance, too, in the debate.

As we stand at bedsides, give us wisdom to answer correctly. Life is too precious to hoard *or* relinquish without prayerful debate. Be in discussions; guide conversations; winnow motives; and restrain tempers. Make sure we are scrupulous about *whose* quality of life we're concerned with, *who* gets to decide, how we decide.

As we ponder how to navigate final wearing-out illnesses that nibble at the heels of aging loved ones, inspire us with their persistence and ingenuity at *bringing* quality to life.

Help us to understand why they keep going as long as possible, why some put bird feeders outside nursing-home windows, why they fight illness's lure, why they endure limitations to keep going. Inspire us with their example. Let us celebrate with them the smallest *quality* moments.

And when *they* decide that *quality of life* is now best spent in reunion with you, Lord, welcome them as enthusiastically as they have welcomed each day of your creation, giving a quality to ours in the doing.

Words to Hold You: "For you shall go out in joy, and be led forth in peace" (Isaiah 55:12a, RSV).

Butterflies: A Hospice Home

We are grateful when there are enough hospice beds to go around, Lord, for they are the first stop on the way to reunion after a good death, the essence of the word, the gift of healing.

Nurses welcome all of us, patient, family, friends, with open arms to this home away from home. With open hearts, they greet questions, grief, and their tasks of tending to the dying as a calling from you.

I felt you guiding my walk through these hospice halls the day I discovered that tiny butterflies were cleverly painted somewhere in every painting: creation, re-creation. It's possible to become part of this process in loving hospice hands. I thank you again with each butterfly I see.

In the hospice home we feel your presence in the care extended, the skill provided to ease last days. "At last," patient and families sigh in relief, "at last we've found a place where it is OK to grieve and go . . . and go on."

Bless these special caregivers who know that death is the final healing, not failure of medicine or personal willpower, and as such rates top-notch, loving attention. Bless their tending of those who wait, multiplying stress with their own needs for comfort, knowledge, permission to go for a walk or to supper . . . to prepare for going on alone.

And when hospice makes house calls, Lord, it transforms gloomy rooms into the comfort of our home, sweet, home en route to yours. It is easier to find our way there when led by butterflies of hope forward through your open door.

Words to Hold You: "You will not be afraid of the terror by night. . . . 'I will be with him in trouble; I will rescue him . . .'" (Psalm 91:5-15, NASB).

Hint of a Rainbow

Our special one is gone, Lord. Period. There is nothing else to say; death has had the last word.

What now is there to live for since there are no plans to make, no dreams to share, no milestones to anticipate? What is strong enough to pull us from beneath the bedcovers each morning? What is there to put in this void once filled with sunlight and promise?

Nothing, Lord; our world is all darkness and shadow. Period.

Yet we sense we cannot stay in this void that looms like an empty pot at the end of a faded rainbow. Help us to see glimmers of your promised healing being added to the empty pot each time we see a cloud lift in the sky, each time we smile in memory, each time we think with curiosity about the future.

In your hands our grief-stricken life can become like a prism that creates miniature rainbows on the wall. A prism is just a useless chunk of glass until light passes through it. So, too, is our grief useless as it is. Redeem it into fond memory and renewed living.

And remind us, Lord, that it takes very little sun shining through a storm to create a rainbow, very little light through a prism. Use our tears as the showers. Shine your love on us as the sun and lift up our eyes so we can see even the smallest curves of hope in the lightening sky.

Words to Hold You: "'I will give you the treasures of darkness . . . that you may know that it is I, the LORD . . ., who calls you by your name" (Isaiah 45:3, NASB).

Cat Naps

We're still wondering about life after death, Lord, for the time is growing close when we'll have to let our loved ones go. But *where* will they go? *How* will they go? We hesitantly ask, praying for enlightenment.

Send us answers while we doze beside this bedside. Answer us in our dreams, on our walks in your creation, and even through our daily lives, for some answers are already there, perhaps as close as a tabby cat.

When we watch her with kittens, we understand. Your after-life love for us is a bit like the mama cat's as she carefully picks up her babies in her mouth and carries them to a better, safer place. Is that what you do for your children when they, we, can no longer live here?

Sometimes from this side of the question we find it hard to believe, even as we yearn to, that you would so lovingly pick us up to put us down in a safe place when we die. Reassure us, Lord.

Bless our questions, for they are the only prayers we have in these upside-down days of impending loss and perplexing absence. There are times, though, when we do feel your warmth gently lifting us from this spot of grief to another, kind of like being moved from one nest to another.

We pray this is what death will be too, Lord, simply being moved from one nest to another by a benevolent, watchful Parent. What joy to be so loved, so carefully tended. We relax in your strong grasp.

Words to Hold You: "He will hide me in his shelter; . . . he will set me high upon a rock" (Psalm 27:5, RSV).

Once Upon a Time: Telling Our Tale
(perhaps to read aloud)

Once upon a time when first I knew this dear one, Lord, I never dreamt of good-bye, and I weep to know death is to be the final healing. I thought we'd have more than enough time to finish all that we began.

Be with me as I collect moments from our life together in a prayer-story to give as a bon voyage gift to this special person:

As I sit beside you sharing this last chapter of life as lovingly as we shared the others, I want to tell our story. Fill in the blanks with me:

- *I recall the first time I saw you; you were . . .*
- *How can I look back without recalling the fun we had? I giggle to remember . . .*
- *We've had disagreements too. Remember the one . . . ? I am grateful we never allowed differences to become barriers. Thank God we are both too stubborn for that!*
- *Our time together is a gift from a wise, strong God, and I've seen that same God's Spirit within you even in these dark days. You showed your faith and courage . . .*
- *As I sit with you, I am choosing what I like best about you. It is probably . . .*

I must go now and leave you to rest, safe in the keeping of the God who introduced us. I'll be back. For now, dream of our other adventures pressed like flowers between pages of the scrapbook of our life.

In the days ahead, I will do something special in your honor—maybe plant a tree, walk in the woods, skip stones on the river, walk barefoot in the rain, climb a mountain, ride a train or a merry-go-round—one of those special things you've always loved. As I do, it will almost be as if you are with me, which you will be, written as you are between the lines of my life.

Bless this tale, Lord, for its making has been a gift from you.

Words to Hold You: ". . . we spend our years as a tale that is told" (Psalm 90:9, KJV).